book

1

Learn PC essentials
at the pace that's ideal for you.

cd

2

Immerse yourself in key concepts
with audio, video and simulations plus
activity-oriented learning games
to develop your skills.

survive
&thrive™

web

3

Enter the exciting world of online
learning with your personal
survive&thrive Online Enrollment Key.
Explore further with timely updates.

class

4

Learn from a friendly instructor
and practice important skills with
other survivers&thrivers.

Additional fees may apply.
Enroll at any Gateway store or call 888-852-4821
for a conveniently scheduled class.

Now you can join the more than **2 million people** who have used
survive&thrive to improve the quality of their lives using technology.

Communicate and Connect to
The Internet

Notices

Communicate and Connect to the Internet
is published by
Gateway, Inc.
14303 Gateway Place
Poway, CA 92064

Version 2.0

ISBN: 1-57729-270-7

DATE: 11-4-02

Printed in the United States of America

Distributed in the United States by Gateway, Inc.

Welcome

From the introduction of The Internet in Chapter 1 through troubleshooting in Chapter 14, *Communicate and Connect to the Internet* provides you with what you need to know to discover the online world with your PC. This product is designed to accommodate your learning style, and to make learning easy, interesting, and fun. You can stick to just the bare essentials or learn in greater depth by practicing key skills and applying your new knowledge. Our goal is to show you how technology can enhance your life, provide some fun, and open up new opportunities.

More Than a Book

Communicate and Connect to the Internet is more than a book; it is a blended learning system that also includes interactive CD-ROM and Internet presentations and activities. These tools all work together to provide a truly unique learning experience. The book presents technical information in visual, practical, and understandable ways. The CD-ROM extends the book by providing audio, video, and animated visuals of important concepts. Continue learning online by logging on to www.LearnwithGateway.com. The enrollment key provided with this book gives you access to additional content and interactive exercises, as well as reference links, Internet resources, and Frequently Asked Questions (FAQs) with answers. This Web site allows us to keep you updated on rapidly changing information and new software releases.

Classroom Learning

In addition, a hands-on training course is offered. Additional fees may apply. Our classes are ideal solutions for people who want to become knowledgeable and get up and running in just three hours. They provide the opportunity to learn from one of our experienced and friendly instructors and practice important skills with other students. Call 888-852-4821 for enrollment information. One of our representatives will assist you in selecting a time and location that is convenient for you. If applicable, please have your Gateway customer ID and order number ready when you call. Please refer to your Gateway paperwork for this information.

Gateway™

Learning map for
Communicate and Connect to
The Internet

This map shows how the elements of Gateway's learning system work for you. The best of an easy to understand, highly visual book, the Internet and CD-ROM are all brought together to give you a unique and truly enjoyable learning experience. Notice how the interactive CD-ROM and Internet activities extend and complement the chapters in the book. Icons in the book will direct you to each element at the proper time.

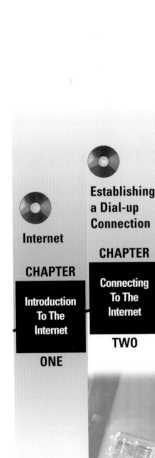

Search Engines Overview
IE6 Favorites: Adding Web Pages
Netscape Bookmarks: Adding Web Pages

Anti-virus Software
Security: Risks and Solutions
IE6: Downloading Files

AOL:
Navigating the Web
Adding Web Pages to Favorites
Downloading Files

E-mail:
Setting Up Accounts
Sending
Replying
Using Attachments

IE6: Navigating the Web
Netscape: Navigating the Web

CHAPTER
Communicating With Family & Friends
EIGHT

CHAPTE
Communicating Through AOL
NINE

CHAPTER
Exploring AOL And The Internet
SEVEN

CHAPTER
Down-Loading From The Internet
SIX

CHAPTER
Searching The Internet
FIVE

CHAPTER
Doing More Online
FOUR

Digital Certificates
Privacy Settings

Establishing a Dial-up Connection

CHAPTER
Browsers And Web Addresses
THREE

IE6:
Overview
Interface
Navigating the Web
Netscape:
Introduction
Navigating the Web

Internet

CHAPTER
Introduction To The Internet
ONE

CHAPTER
Connecting To The Internet
TWO

IE6:
Organizing Favorites
Save Options
Setting Page Options
Printing a Web Page
Saving a Web Page
Netscape:
Saving a Web Page
Printing a Web Page

AOL:
Introduction
Connecting
Navigating the Web
Companion
Help
Favorites
Keywords

E-mail:
Using Contacts
Opening
Saving

Download Files
E-mail Messages
Sending
Replying
Adding Attachme
Compiling an Addre Book

You can also take a Gateway℠ class,
and this is an ideal way to continue
to expand your learning. Gateway
instructors are dedicated to
working with each individual and
answering all your questions. You
will be able to talk with other
learners, practice important skills,
and get off to a quick start.
Additional fees may apply.
Call 888-852-4821 to enroll.
See you in class!

Contents

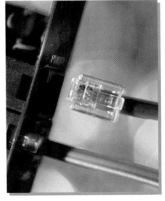

Contents

Contents

Contents

Contents

How To Use This Book

As you read the chapters in this book, you'll find pictures, figures, and diagrams to help reinforce key ideas and concepts. You'll also find numerous pictures, or icons, that serve as cues to flag important information or provide directions. Here is a guide to help you understand the icons you'll encounter in this book:

 A Note identifies a relatively important piece of information that will make things easier or faster for you to accomplish on your PC. Most notes are worth reading, if only for the time and effort they can save you.

 A Warning gives notice that an action on your PC can have serious consequences and could lead to loss of work, delays, or other problems. Our goal is not to scare you, but to steer you clear of potential sources of trouble.

 The CD-ROM flags additional materials including exercises and animations that you will find on the CD-ROM included with this book. Because some materials work better on your PC than in print, we've included many activities and exercises. These help you become more familiar with your system while practicing important skills.

 Because PC information and online resources are so dynamic, some material related to this book, including Web-based training, resides on the **www.LearnwithGateway.com** Web site. This allows us to keep that information fresh and up to date.

 The *Survive & Thrive* series includes several books on topics from digital music to the Internet. Where other titles can be useful in improving and expanding your learning, we use the Book icon to draw those titles to your attention.

 Gateway offers a hands-on training course on many of the topics covered in this book. Additional fees may apply. Call 888-852-4821 for enrollment information. If applicable, please have your customer ID and order number ready when you call.

You'll find sidebar information sprinkled throughout the chapters, as follows:

More About . . .

The More About . . . information is supplementary, and is provided so you can learn more about making technology work for you. Feel free to skip this material during your first pass through the book, but please return to it later.

Introduction to the Internet

Y ou've probably heard a lot about the Internet, even if you're not sure exactly what it is or what it can offer you. It's difficult to pick up a newspaper, listen to the radio, or watch television without seeing or hearing some reference to the Internet. Often called the "information superhighway," the Internet has been described in many different ways. It's been called everything from a vast storehouse of information to an online profit center where products and services can be bought and sold.

No matter how it's characterized, there's no doubt that the Internet has made a significant impact on our lives. It's changed the way many people shop, conduct business, learn, communicate with friends and family, and more. It has become so popular that a lot of people actually buy personal computers (PCs) just to connect to the Internet.

This book introduces you to the Internet. It helps you understand what you need to know to do things *online*, which means you're connected to the Internet. This chapter gives you a little background about the Internet, describes the variety of material available online, and introduces you to what you can use the Internet for.

Getting to Know the Internet

Simply put, the *Internet* is a global network of computers designed to share information and support communication. But even this simple definition includes a few items that need clarifying. A *network* is two or more computers connected by communication devices, such as a phone line or a cable and a NIC (network interface card), so that they

can exchange files and other data. When you share information over the Internet, you use a computer to send a file (such as a document, a picture, a sound file, a movie file, a software program, and more) to another computer. Similarly, the Internet supports communication by allowing one computer to send some form of message (such as text, computer code, audio, video, and more) to another computer.

There are other definitions that offer more details and begin to reveal the complexity of the Internet. For example, the Internet is not just a single, large network; rather, it's made up of thousands and thousands of smaller networks. Each network is connected to other networks, which creates the communication pathways needed to move data and messages from one system to another.

Think of the Internet as a forest: A forest looks like one big entity when viewed from a significant distance, such as from an airplane flying overhead. But it's not a single entity; it's comprised of thousands of individual trees of all shapes and sizes. The trees in a forest often touch each other with their outstretched branches. A squirrel can scamper from one tree to another to another, maybe even travel across the entire forest, just as a message or a file can be transmitted from one computer to another over the Internet.

The United States Department of Defense laid the foundation for the Internet in 1969 when it developed a communications network as a security measure. The network was created with numerous communication paths across which messages and information could travel between one computer and another. If one path was damaged or destroyed, others remained available. In the late 1980s, the NSF (National Science Foundation) hooked its network of five *supercomputers* (very large, complex computers) into the defense network. Realizing the potential of this technology, businesses, institutions, and individuals began setting up their own smaller networks and connecting them to the already existing network. By the 1990s, the Internet had grown into a worldwide public community in which personal, educational, business, and government activities occurred simultaneously.

Today, the Internet is a global network connecting millions of computers. When you go online, you're connecting your computer to this widespread network, and in turn, you're able to access the Internet's numerous information resources. The information you view could be stored on a computer in San Francisco, Paris, or Hong Kong. You'll probably never know where the computer is located. What matters to you is that the information all appears in the same place—on your computer screen—and that it's all right at your fingertips. The Internet is a virtual worldwide treasure chest that is constantly changing and ready for you to explore!

 Although there's a lot of useful, educational information on the Internet, remember that there may also be some undesirable information. This book will help you figure out how to steer clear of it!

The Internet is not just a repository of data; it also enables quick, efficient, almost effortless communication between people no matter where they are geographically located. The Internet has effectively transformed our multination planet into a single global community. Two of the most popular communication mechanisms used on the Internet are e-mail and chat. We'll take a close look at e-mail in Chapters 8 and 9, and we'll explore chat in Chapters 10 and 11.

Learning What the Internet Has to Offer

When you go online, you're connecting to the Internet, which gives you access to Web sites, e-mail (electronic mail), databases, computer networks, and much more. The Internet has changed the way we communicate with friends, family, and even co-workers by bridging the distances that once divided us. It has dramatically changed the ways in which we receive our news, do our banking, shop, play games, learn about new things, work, make travel reservations, meet new people, and more. The Internet seems to permeate every aspect of our lives.

Although not everyone is online, the online universe offers so much for those who want to use and explore it. You can perform many activities online, just a few of which are listed here:

- ✦ Send and receive e-mail

- ✦ Read newspapers, magazines, and other information

- ✦ Research medical problems

- ✦ Access entire books or libraries

- ✦ Check the weather and local news

- ✦ Read product reviews and evaluations

- ✦ Follow sporting events, scores, teams, statistics, and more

- ✦ Make travel plans, such as airline, hotel, cruise, and car rental reservations

- Play online multiplayer games

- Download computer programs, pictures, and music

- Browse stores and buy products

- Shop for groceries

- Attend "virtual" live concerts, sporting events, plays, or other special events

- Communicate with others via audio/video conferencing

- Chat with others in real time

- Research family history or find long-lost friends or schoolmates

- Download federal and state tax forms and even pay your taxes

You can find information relating to just about anything on the Internet, which is what makes it truly amazing!

In later chapters of this book, we explore several of these activities, such as shopping, looking for a job, researching topics, accessing child-safe content, searching for information, downloading files, using e-mail, chatting, and more. But before you can do any of that, you must have an account with an ISP (Internet service provider) or online service company.

To gain an overview of the World Wide Web and key terminology, go to the CD-ROM segment *Internet*.

Defining the World Wide Web

The Internet and World Wide Web are often mistakenly thought to be the same thing. The Internet is actually a physical network; a connection that exists between millions of computers around the world, allowing them to communicate back and forth. Thus, when you connect your computer to the Internet, you're linking it your neighbors' computers (if they're connected to the Internet), as well as to the computers of Internet users around the world.

The *World Wide Web* (often just called the Web), however, is a vast collection of interconnected graphical and textual information that exists because the Internet provides a foundation for it. A lot of the content found on the Web comes from schools, companies, governments, and professional groups, but some of it comes from individuals just like you.

Although the Web may get most of the attention and visibility, it's just one among many services, communities, and resources that the Internet offers. Of these, the best known is the America Online® service (AOL), where millions of individuals meet daily to chat, exchange ideas and information, and much more.

To access the Web, you typically use software called a *Web browser*—also called a *browser* for short. If your computer is running Microsoft® Windows® XP, you already have a browser—Internet Explorer, shown in Figure 1-1. Internet Explorer is Microsoft's premier browser and is one of the most widely used browsers on the Internet. You can also use numerous other browsers, including Netscape Navigator® and Opera.

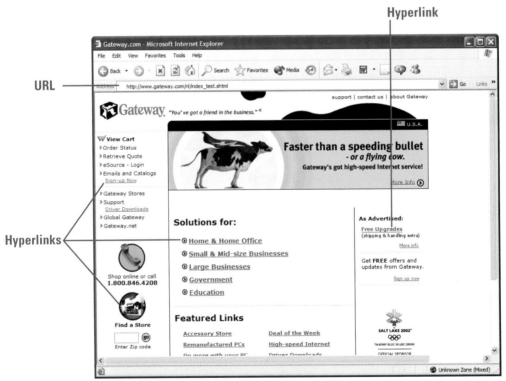

Figure 1-1 Internet Explorer, a Web browser.

Some ISPs and online services, such as the America Online service, have their own customized browser designed to focus your attention on and grant you access to exclusive content and specialized features. A discussion of other browsers is included in Chapter 3.

Web browsers enable you to view Web sites, such as the Gateway site shown in Figure 1-1. A *Web site* is a collection of online documents that is maintained by a group or an individual and that addresses one or more topics. A Web site might be about someone's cat, a new bicycle model, a new product, a business, or almost anything else you could imagine. Web sites can include pictures, sounds, and even animation and video clips. Some Web sites offer downloadable programs and products for you to purchase.

A Web site is made up of one or more Web pages. A *Web page* is a document formatted for viewing over the Internet through a Web browser. A specialized language called a *markup language* is used to create Web pages by defining the layout of the text and graphics. The one most commonly used is called HTML (Hypertext Markup Language). A Web page usually includes links, called hyperlinks, to other Web pages or Web sites. *Hyperlinks* are text or graphical elements on a Web page that you can click to go to another Web page. Links normally appear in a different color than the surrounding text and are usually underlined. The underlined text in Figure 1-2 represents hyperlinks.

As shown in Figure 1-2, when you move your mouse pointer over a hyperlink, the pointer changes from an arrow to a hand with a pointing finger.

Figure 1-2 A hyperlink being selected.

A hyperlink connects you to another Web site or another page within a Web site by supplying your browser with a special kind of Internet address known as a *URL (Uniform Resource Locator)*. In addition, you go to other Web sites by entering URLs into your browser's address bar. (See Chapter 3 for more on how to do this.) Here are some examples of URLs:

+ http://www.gateway.com

+ http://www.microsoft.com/windowsxp/

+ http://www.yahoo.com

+ http://www.ebay.com

+ http://www.amazon.com

+ http://www.half.com

+ http://ask.com

Chapter 3 includes a detailed discussion of what a URL is, how a URL is constructed, and how to use one.

A *home page* identifies a predefined Web site that your Web browser loads each time it opens. It's common practice to set your home page to display local news, local weather, or something else of personal interest. For example, many companies set up their employees' Web browsers to open to the company Web site. You'll also find that many ISPs and online services will preconfigure your Web browser to load their preferred custom home page when you sign up for their service.

A *Web server* is a computer on the Internet that houses one or more Web sites. Web browsers communicate with Web servers to access Web pages. The browser manages the transfer of elements (text, graphics, and so forth) that result in a Web page on your monitor screen.

We've thrown a lot of terms your way in this section, but now we're going to provide an analogy for you that will make all these terms crystal clear. Imagine your cable TV provider as the *Web server*, your remote control as the *Web browser*, the different channels you have access to as the *Web sites*, and the different programs on each channel as the *Web pages*. You'll notice that there's not an analogy for hyperlinks here though. That's because the hyperlinks are what make the Web unique!

Now that you have a basic understanding of the Internet and the World Wide Web, it's time you learn how to get connected to the Internet. The next chapter walks you through the process of getting connected.

TO KEEP ON LEARNING . . .

Go to the CD-ROM and select the segment:
- ◆ *Internet* to gain an overview of the World Wide Web and key terminology.

Go online to **www.LearnwithGateway.com** and log on to select:
- ◆ *Internet Links and Resources*
- ◆ *FAQs*

With the *Survive & Thrive* series, refer to *Use and Care for Your PC* for more information on:
- ◆ *Networking*

Gateway offers a hands-on training course that covers many of the topics in this chapter. Additional fees may apply. Call **888-852-4821** for enrollment information. If applicable, please have your customer ID and order number ready when you call.

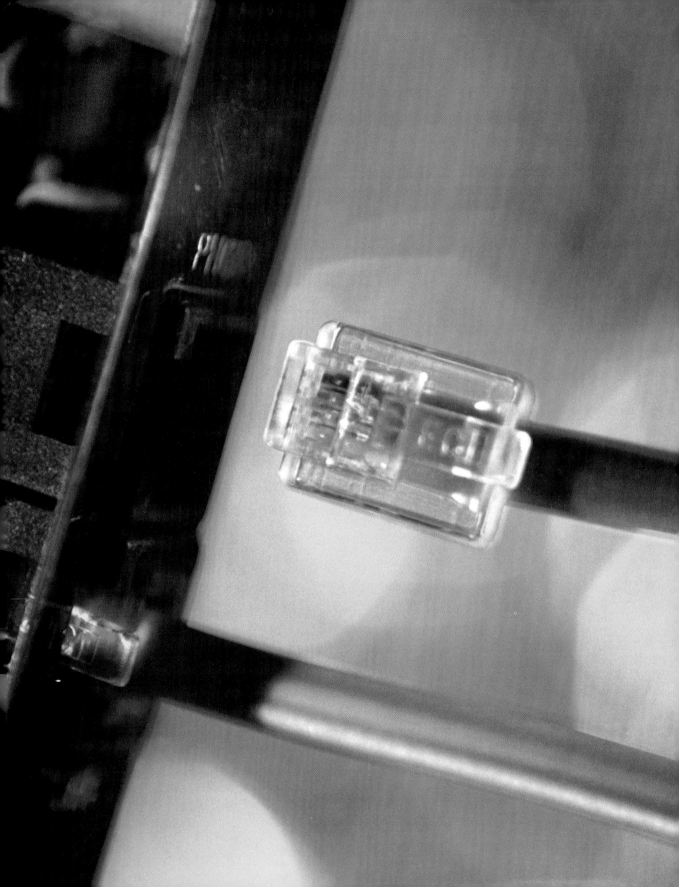

Connecting to the Internet

R emember the mixture of anxiety and excitement you felt the first time you drove a car? A lot of people feel the same way when they connect their computer to the Internet for the first time—they want to do it, but they're afraid they might somehow make a mistake or fail altogether. If you figured out how to drive a car (or learned how to ride a bike, for that matter), there's good news: connecting to the Internet is a lot easier!

Establishing your Internet connection for the first time doesn't have to be a daunting task. In this chapter, we'll look at a few of the most popular means to connect to the Internet. We'll discuss how you find an ISP (Internet service provider) or online service and the steps necessary to get connected. Once you're set up properly, getting online is painless.

Choosing Communication Devices

To connect to the Internet, you'll need a special kind of hardware, called a *communication device*, which allows your computer to exchange data with other computers. There are many kinds of communication devices, and it's important that you choose the appropriate one for the kind of Internet connection you have. If you plan to connect to the Internet using a standard phone line, for example, you'll need a modem, which is sometimes already installed in your computer when you buy it. Other communication hardware, such as a cable modem, is external and is connected to various ports in your computer.

Modems

As noted previously, a *modem* is a device that allows a computer (sometimes called a personal computer, or PC) to communicate or exchange data with other computers using a standard phone line. The modem dials out over the telephone line to establish a connection to the Internet. A modem can be an expansion card already installed inside your computer (see Figure 2-1) or an external device connected to a computer via a serial cable.

Modem and phone cord

 Modems that communicate over regular phone lines offer maximum connection speed of 56 Kbps.

Figure 2-1 A typical expansion-card modem with connected phone cord.

Because modems are the most common and widely used type of Internet connection, this book focuses on using them. However, other than the initial configuration process, connecting to and using the Internet is pretty much the same no matter which type of communication device you use.

More About . . . Communication Speeds

The speed at which a communication device, such as a modem, sends and receives data is called its *throughput*. The amount of data that can be sent or received by a communication device within a specific amount of time depends on its throughput capabilities.

Three common measurement terms are used to describe throughput: *Kbps* (kilobits per second), *Mbps* (megabits per second), and *Gbps* (gigabits per second). A bit is a single binary digit of a 1 or a 0. Kbps is equal to 1,024 bps. Mbps is 1,024 Kbps, or 1,024,000 bits. Gbps is 1,024 Mbps, or 1,024,000,000 bits.

Notice that a lowercase *b* is used to describe throughput speed, whereas an uppercase *B* is used to describe hard-drive capacity, as in KB (kilobytes), MB (megabytes), and GB (gigabytes). The lowercase *b* stands for *bits*, and the uppercase *B* stands for *bytes*. There are 8 bits in a byte, so it would take about 8 seconds to transmit a 1 MB file over a 1 Mbps connection.

Cable Modems

To connect to the Internet using a high-speed broadband Internet service, you need a *cable modem* (see Figure 2-2). Many cable television companies, such as Time Warner Road Runner and AT&T Broadband, offer high-speed broadband Internet service, or cable Internet service as it's often called. Cable Internet service typically offers very fast throughput capabilities—up to 2 Mbps for downloading data and 300 Kbps for uploading data. It's a shared medium, however, which means that if many people in your neighborhood use their cable modem connections at the same time, everyone's connection runs slower. Cable modems are typically external devices that connect to a computer through a network interface card (discussed later in this chapter).

Figure 2-2 A typical cable modem.

  Cable Internet service is not available in all areas. Check with your local cable company to see if the service is available where you live.

DSL Modems

DSL (digital subscriber line) modems (see Figure 2-3) use a new feature of digital telephone service to provide high-speed Internet access. Your local telephone company must have specific hardware in your area, and your house must be located within a certain distance from the switching station where DSL access is made available to local subscribers.

 Check with your local telephone company to see if it offers DSL service. It's not available in all areas.

Figure 2-3 A typical DSL modem.

A DSL connection uses a phone line but allows you to place and receive calls while connected to the Internet. DSL connections typically offer 384 Kbps to 1.5 Mbps for downloading data and 128 Kbps for uploading data. The real benefit of DSL is that it's a dedicated medium. In other words, unlike a high-speed broadband connection, the presence of other DSL users in your neighborhood won't affect your upload and download speeds. DSL modems are either expansion cards installed inside the computer or external devices connected to a network interface card.

Network Interface Cards

A computer connects to a network using a *NIC* (network interface card), which is also sometimes called a *network adapter* (see Figure 2-4) and is pronounced "Nick." As noted in Chapter 1, a network allows multiple computers to share files, printers, data, and even Internet connections. The issues related to networking are beyond the scope of this book; suffice it to say that a NIC permits a computer to access a network and, because some networks are themselves connected to the Internet, to use that connection for Internet access as well.

DSL or cable modems are often connected to a computer via a NIC. So, even if you aren't connected to a network, your computer may have a NIC so it can connect to a high-speed communication device.

Figure 2-4 A typical NIC.

Setting Up an Internet Account

The first step in getting connected to the Internet is to find an ISP or online service. An ISP or an online service can be a local provider or a national company. If you're not sure what company to use, ask the employees of your local computer store to recommend one. Alternatively, check your local newspaper or yellow pages, or contact your community's Chamber of Commerce. Many people elect to establish accounts with their local phone company, local cable television company, or well-known national providers like the America Online service (also called AOL).

Getting Started

To go online using a dial-up connection, most users need the following basic items:

✦ **A modem.** A *modem* is a device that communicates with other computers over a standard phone line.

 If you find yourself spending lots of time online and don't mind spending a bit more money, consider using a DSL or cable modem connection instead. These connection technologies offer speeds 10 to 100 times faster than the best phone modems.

✦ **A telephone line.** You'll need a standard telephone line to connect a modem to an ISP or online service. You can use your existing phone line, but that interferes with normal use of your home phone. For example, if you're online but need to make a telephone call, you'll have to disconnect from the Internet. Alternatively, people trying to call you while you're online may get a busy signal or interrupt your connection. If you use a modem to go online frequently, consider adding a second phone line for your computer. A dedicated phone line for your computer doesn't need call waiting, caller ID, call forwarding, or any other special feature—you can even disable long-distance dialing on it.

✦ **An ISP or online service account.** An *ISP* or *online service account* is a service contract with an Internet service provider or online service that defines what type of connection may be used and how many hours the connection can be active per month before extra charges apply. Service contracts come in many shapes and sizes. For example, some service contracts are month to month, whereas others may be purchased yearly. Additionally, some service contracts limit the amount of time you can be connected or the amount of data you can download. Be sure to read your contract's fine print before signing on with an ISP or online service.

 To learn more about connecting to the Internet, go to the CD-ROM segment *Dial-up Connections: Establishing.*

More About . . . ISPs and Online Services

The America Online service is a community composed of millions of people with different interests and backgrounds. Using the America Online service, you can communicate with other members using e-mail, AOL® Instant Messenger™, chat rooms, and public message boards. You can also obtain vast amounts of information on varying subjects. In addition to all the offerings you have within the AOL community, you can access all the wonders and riches outside of that community on the Internet.

The America Online service offers one of the fastest and easiest ways for you to access everything the Internet has to offer. With the America Online service as your Internet online service, you can get the following features:

✦ An Internet online service that's easy to get started and easy to use

✦ Unlimited Internet access with fast connection speeds

✦ Easy-to-use e-mail, AOL Instant Messenger, and the Buddy List® feature to keep in touch with all your friends and family

✦ Free, 24-hour customer service, on the phone or online, to help you anytime

✦ Up to seven e-mail addresses for every America Online service account

✦ The "You've Got Pictures" feature to share your photos online

✦ Parental Controls that help safeguard your kids online

✦ Shop@AOL and AOL's 100 percent Guarantee of Satisfaction that takes the worry out of online shopping

For more information about the America Online service, check out Chapters 7, 9, 11, and 13.

Configuring Your Account

After you have a service contract with an ISP or online service, you're ready to set up your account. This involves setting certain controls on your computer, or configuring it to dial into the ISP or online service. Many ISPs and online services, such as the America Online service, simplify this process by providing new customers with an installation disk that performs all configurations for them; others might provide step-by-step instructions instead.

 If you need more information about configuring your computer, don't hesitate to ask your ISP or online service. A typical service contract entitles you to ask for help so you can use the connection you pay for.

The process of setting up an account with an ISP or online service differs for each provider. Even so, there are certain steps you must take to get online no matter which ISP or online service you decide to use:

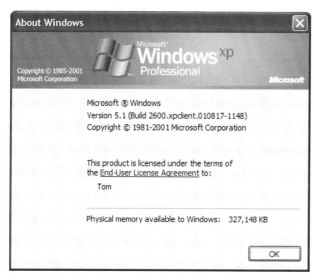

① Identify your operating system. Be sure you know what operating system is on your computer because configuration settings differ for each operating system. If you're not sure how to identify your operating system, click the start button, click Run, type winver, and click OK. A message box appears and lists the version of your operating system.

② Install the modem. If your computer did not come with a modem preinstalled, you'll need to install one yourself—be sure to install the modem's driver on your computer as well. Also, make sure the telephone line is properly connected to the modem and the wall outlet.

 A *driver* is a special type of software that allows a specific hardware device to communicate with your computer. For example, the operating system requires a printer driver to interact with a printer attached to a computer.

③ **Install the software.** If the ISP or online service software comes preinstalled on your computer, you should be able to launch the setup procedure from the start menu or from a desktop icon. Otherwise, if the ISP provided you software, you'll have to install it.

④ **Obtain the access phone number.** You'll need the phone number of the ISP or online service at some point during setup. Some preinstalled software packages use a built-in toll-free number at first, but ultimately require you to choose a local dial-up number from a list that the ISP or online service provides. If you use a local ISP or online service, it provides you with one or more working phone numbers for dial-up access.

⑤ **Select membership options and/or payment information.** Some ISPs and online services require you to define membership settings and payment options the first time you connect. Other ISPs and online services handle such settings offline when you first contact them. Either way, you must supply this information at some point.

 If your ISP or online service offers multiple payment plans or membership options, take time to evaluate each one to see how it fits your budget and expected usage. Don't worry if you get a plan that offers too few hours; ISP and online services are happy to sign you up for more services.

⑥ **Agree to conditions of membership.** You must read and agree to some sort of user license, acceptable-use policy, or conditions-of-membership document before your ISP or online service will grant you online access.

 Be sure you read the user license carefully before you sign it or agree to it. Usually, it's there to protect the ISP or online service from any illegal activities that users may conduct, but it might also tell you if the ISP or online service monitors your access activities or under what circumstances the company might show your e-mail to authorities.

⑦ **Choose account name and password.** Some ISPs and online services assign you an account name (or user name) and a password rather than allowing you to create your own. In some cases, your account name serves as your primary e-mail address. Be sure to record your account name and password; these are required to establish a dial-up connection to your ISP or online service.

More About . . . Online Accounts

Some ISPs and online services, such as the America Online service, require you to set up a *primary master account* or a *master screen name.* This account is used to establish a connection between your computer and the ISP or online service. After you've completed the setup and initial-connection process, you can create *secondary* or *individual accounts.* Other family members can use these secondary accounts to establish their own e-mail addresses and online identities. Although ISPs and online services may limit the number of secondary accounts within one primary master account, there's usually no additional charge for these accounts.

Internet Connection Step-by-Step

Your ISP or online service should provide you with detailed step-by-step instructions on how to get connected using a dial-up connection if that's what you have. If it didn't, we've included a set of generic instructions that will work for most dial-up situations if you're using Windows XP.

Before starting, gather the following pieces of information:

✦ The access phone number of the ISP or online service

✦ Your account name

✦ Your account password

Next, perform the following steps:

1. Make sure you're logged on to your system as a computer administrator.
2. Open Control Panel by clicking the start button and selecting Control Panel. Control Panel window opens.

 These are the steps if you're in Category View. If you're in Classic View instead, open Control Panel and double-click the Internet Options icon to open the Internet Properties dialog box (see step 4).

3 Click **Network and Internet Connections**. The Network and Internet Connections window opens.

4 Click **Set up or change your Internet connection**. The Internet Properties dialog box opens.

5 If necessary, click the **Connections** tab.

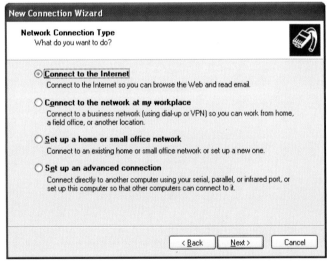

6 Click **Setup**. The New Connection Wizard appears.

7 Click **Next**. The Network Connection Type screen of the New Connection Wizard appears.

8 Select the radio button labeled **Connect to the Internet** and then click **Next**. The Getting Ready screen of the New Connection Wizard appears.

9 Select the radio button labeled **Set up my connection manually**. (The other two options are typically used when you follow the instructions given to you by an ISP or online service provider.)

10 Click **Next**. The Internet Connection screen of the New Connection Wizard appears.

11 Select the radio button labeled **Connect using a dial-up modem** and then click **Next**. The Connection Name screen of the New Connection Wizard appears.

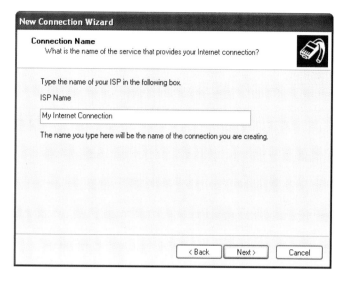

⑫ In the ISP Name text field, type the name of the ISP or online service or any other name you'd like to use to identify this Internet connection (such as My Internet Connection).

⑬ Click Next. The Phone Number to Dial screen of the New Connection Wizard appears.

⑭ In the Phone number text field, type the dial-up phone number for the ISP or online service. If you need to dial the area code or other dialing prefixes, be sure to include them here.

⑮ Click Next. The Internet Account Information screen of the New Connection Wizard appears.

⑯ In the text field labeled User name, type your account user name. In the text field labeled Password, type your account password. In the text field labeled Confirm password, type your password again. For security purposes, you'll see dots instead of the letters you type in both of the password fields. There are three check boxes on this screen that should remain marked in most cases:

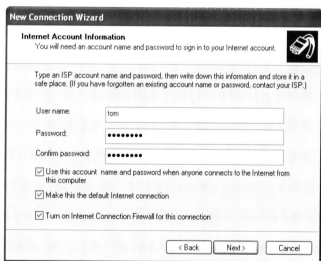

✦ If this Internet connection is to be used only by a single person (the person currently logged in), clear the check box labeled Use this account name and password when anyone connects to the Internet from this computer.

✦ If this Internet connection is the primary and/or only Internet connection, select the check box labeled Make this the default Internet connection.

✦ Unless you specifically don't want to use the built-in firewall to protect this Internet connection, select the check box labeled Turn on Internet Connection Firewall for this connection.

A firewall is a piece of software or hardware that can selectively block access to your computer from unauthorized outsiders.

⑰ Click Next. The Completing the New Connection Wizard screen of the New Connection Wizard appears.

⑱ Click Finish.

⑲ Click the Close button (the button with the X in the upper-right corner) to close the Network and Internet Connections window.

At this point, you've defined your Internet connection. This activity has added a new item called Connect To to your start menu just below the Control Panel item. The Connect To start menu item is a menu of Internet connections. To open your Internet connection, click the start button, select Connect To, and then select the name of your Internet connection (the name you defined in step 12).

When you launch your Internet connection, a Connect dialog box opens (see Figure 2-5). This dialog box shows the user name, phone number, and other settings for this Internet connection. Click Dial to initiate the connection process. It might take several moments for the connection to be fully established. You might hear strange noises from the speakers or the back of your computer. You'll see a progress window showing what the computer is doing, starting with dialing, then verifying user name and password, and finally registering your computer with the network (the ISP's Internet network in this case).

Figure 2-5 The Connect dialog box showing the details for the Internet connection described in this chapter.

After the connection is established, a new icon—two computer monitors—appears in the notification area of the taskbar. You'll also see a ToolTip that states that you're now connected and shows the speed of the connection. As data is sent or received over this link, the screens of the two monitors blink. As long as your Internet connection is active, open, or live, you can send e-mails, surf the Web, download files, and so on.

Connection icon

 Don't be alarmed if the ToolTip shows that the speed of your connection is below 56 Kbps; you'll usually see a value of around 28.8 Kbps. This doesn't mean your modem is working slower than it's supposed to.

Disconnect command ———

To terminate an Internet connection, right-click the connection icon and select Disconnect from the shortcut menu.

Configuring Automatic Connections

Fortunately, you don't have to manually establish your Internet connection every time you want to use it. That would be like having to set the time and channel preferences on your VCR every time you wanted to record something. Instead, you can configure your computer to automatically dial your Internet connection anytime you want access to Internet resources. To configure your computer to dial your default Internet connection automatically, perform the following steps:

1. Make sure you're logged on to your system as a computer administrator.
2. Open Control Panel by clicking the start button, and selecting Control Panel. Control Panel window opens.
3. Click Network and Internet Connections. The Network and Internet Connections window opens.
4. Click Internet Options. The Internet Properties dialog box opens.

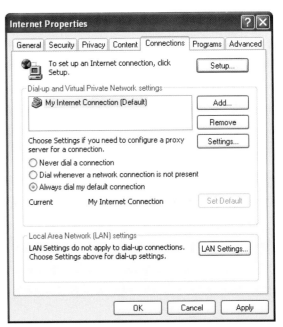

5. If necessary, click the Connections tab.
6. Select the radio button labeled Always dial my default connection and then click OK.
7. Click the Close button to close the Network and Internet Connections window.

Now your computer will automatically dial your Internet connection anytime access to an Internet resource is required. When you use a Web browser to access a Web page, an e-mail program to send or receive e-mail, or any other type of Internet tool, your computer automatically connects to your ISP or online service to open your Internet connection.

Configuring E-mail and Chat

Congratulations! You're almost ready to connect to and use the Internet. If you were learning to drive a car, you would only need to set the radio dials to your favorite stations and make sure the seat is adjusted properly before you turn the key and shift into drive. All you need to do before you're ready to take off on the information superhighway is configure your e-mail and chat programs.

 Your Web browser is essentially already properly configured the moment you complete the steps in the preceding section. So, there's nothing else required before you start surfing the Web. However, there is a lot to know about surfing and using Web browsers. If you'll read Chapters 3-6, you'll find out what to do, how to do it, and where to find information online.

Configuring your e-mail program is not especially difficult, but it does require precision. You'll need to define your e-mail user account name (which is not always your dial-up account name), your associated password, your e-mail address, and the addresses of the inbound and outbound e-mail servers. Don't worry; we provide information on this in Chapter 8.

As for other Internet tools, such as chat, sometimes detailed configuration is required and sometimes it isn't. It all depends on what the tool does and how it finds what it needs on the Internet. We look at chat tools and a few common configurations in Chapter 10.

If you want to use an Internet tool that we don't cover in this book, the user manual for a program usually has setup/configuration instructions. The user manual for software is sometimes a printed booklet, sometimes it's an electronic help file, and other times it's a Web site.

Go to the CD-ROM and select the segment:

✦ *Dial-up Connections: Establishing* to learn more about connecting to the Internet.

Go online to **www.LearnwithGateway.com** and log on to select:

✦ *Internet Links and Resources*

✦ *FAQs*

With the *Survive & Thrive* series, refer to *Use and Care for Your PC* for more information on:

✦ *Using application windows and dialog boxes*

✦ *Logging on as administrator*

Gateway offers a hands-on training course that covers many of the topics in this chapter. Additional fees may apply. Call **888-852-4821** for enrollment information. If applicable, please have your customer ID and order number ready when you call.

CHAPTER **3**

Browsers and Web Addresses

After you've set up an account with an ISP (Internet service provider) or online service (discussed in Chapter 2), all you need to start surfing the Web is a Web browser and a basic understanding of how to use it. This is good news because the Web has been called the largest library ever. And there's even better news: You probably already have a Web browser on your computer—every version of the Windows operating system comes with one. Don't worry if, for some reason, you don't have a browser, because they're easy to get and they're free! In this chapter, you'll learn about Web browsers and their basic controls.

Introducing Web Browsers

A Web browser is an essential tool for anyone using the Internet or other online services; just as a steering wheel is an essential tool needed for you to drive your car. You use a browser to control your movement on the Internet. Without one, it's impossible to access the vast amounts of information online—just like it's impossible to get anywhere in your car without your steering wheel.

There are many Web browsers available for Windows XP and other operating systems. Every version of Windows includes Internet Explorer. Internet Explorer is included with Windows XP. However, Internet Explorer is not the only Web browser you can use; other popular browsers include Netscape Navigator (see Figure 3-1) and Opera (see Figure 3-2).

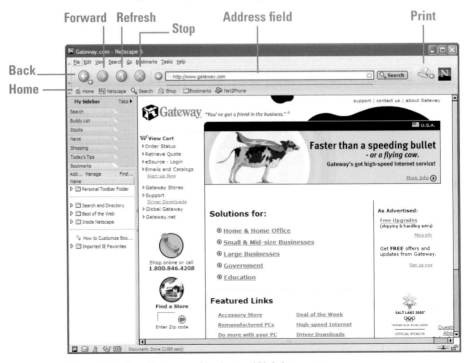

Figure 3-1 The Netscape Navigator Web browser.

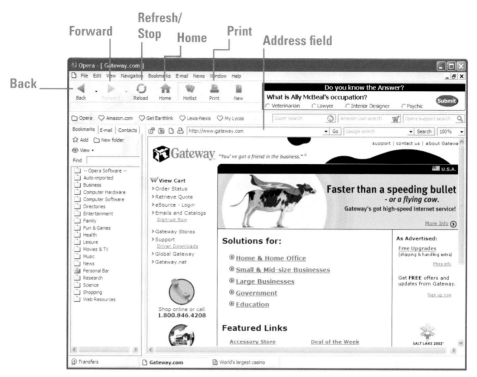

Figure 3-2 The Opera Web browser.

Although every browser has some unique features and capabilities, most share common basic controls for Web browsing, similar to the way the controls in cars vary depending on the make and model of the car. Because you probably already have Internet Explorer on your computer, we'll use it as our primary example and teaching tool in this book. After you learn how to use Internet Explorer, you can apply that knowledge to any other browser.

To see the key features of the Internet Explorer browser, go to the CD-ROM segment *Internet Explorer: Navigating the Web*.

To see the key features of the Netscape Navigator browser, go to the CD-ROM segment *Netscape: Navigating the Web*.

Using Your Web Browser

Let's take a look at the basic Internet Explorer program window. As shown in Figure 3-3, an Internet Explorer window includes all the common program window controls as well as standard browser controls.

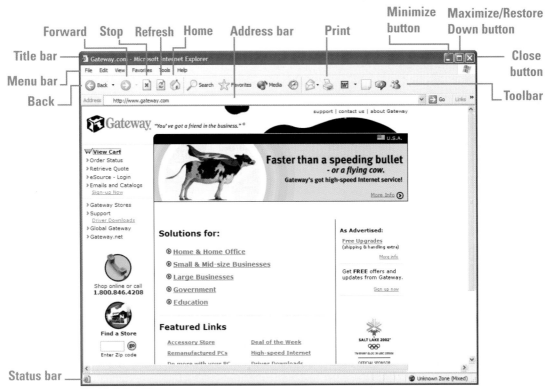

Figure 3-3 Common program window and browser controls in Internet Explorer.

 Refer back to Figures 3-1 and 3-2 to see the visual similarities between Internet Explorer, Netscape Navigator, and Opera. Note the various locations of their common control buttons.

The first, and one of the most notable browser controls, is the Address bar, which displays a URL for the Web page currently on display in the browser. To jump directly to another Web site, you can type its URL in the Address field, replacing what's displayed, and then press ENTER or click Go.

The other common browser controls are shown in Table 3-1.

Table 3-1 Common browser controls.

GRAPHIC	NAME	DESCRIPTION
Back ⌄	Back button	Click the **Back** button once to jump to the Web page you viewed prior to the page currently displayed. Click the **Back** button repeatedly to revisit pages from even earlier in your Web session. In many browsers, the Back button features a small downward-pointing arrow, which you can click to display a list of recently visited pages. To jump to a page in the list, simply click it. If you just opened the browser, the Back button is inactive.
→ ⌄	Forward button	If you've clicked the Back button at least once, the Forward button becomes active. Click it to return to the page you were viewing when you clicked the Back button. Like the Back button, the Forward button in most browsers maintains a drop-down list of recently visited pages.
✕	Stop button	Click the **Stop** button to stop any Web page from loading; for example, a Web page that contains a large graphic that's taking a long time to load. Clicking the Stop button halts all transfer activity but displays all Web page elements that have loaded successfully.
⟳	Refresh button	Click the **Refresh** button to reload the most recent version of the current Web page. This is useful if a page hasn't loaded correctly or if it's a page that changes frequently, such as a stock-ticker page or one that's tracking a live sporting event.
🏠	Home button	Click the **Home** button to load your home page (the page loaded by default when the Web browser is first opened). The Home button offers a convenient way to get to your home page without clicking the Back button repeatedly.
🖨	Print button	Click the **Print** button to print whatever Web page is currently on display.

 The icons that appear in a browser's toolbars to represent these controls may be different from the icons shown here, but their functions are always the same. The icons shown here come from Internet Explorer as it appears in Windows XP.

 To learn more about the Internet Explorer browser, go to the Web segments *Internet Explorer: Overview* and *Internet Explorer: Interface* in the Internet Explorer course.

To learn more about the Netscape browser, go to the Web segment *Netscape Introduction* in the Netscape course.

In addition to button controls, Web browsers offer multiple menu commands. In Internet Explorer, these commands appear in the following menu locations:

✦ **File, Open.** Click this command to access the Open dialog box. This dialog box serves the same function as the Address field; simply type a URL in the Open field and click **OK** to jump to an Internet location.

✦ **File, Print.** This command works almost the same as clicking the Print button on the toolbar, except instead of printing the Web page instantly, the Print command opens a Print dialog box. From there, you can select an alternate printer, choose to print only a certain number of pages, or increase the number of copies printed.

✦ **Edit, Find.** This command opens the Find dialog box, which you can use to search a Web page for a keyword. Just type a keyword or phrase in the Find what field, and click **Find Next**. If the keyword appears on that page, the first instance will be highlighted. (You might need to move the Find dialog box to see the keyword.) To continue searching the page for the same keyword, click **Find Next** again. In Netscape Navigator, use Search, Find in This Page, which works the same as Edit, Find.

♦ **View, Go To.** Click **Go To** in the View menu to choose from a submenu of commands, including Back, Forward, and Home Page. These commands perform the same actions as their toolbar counterparts described earlier in this chapter. The Window menu lists the previously visited URLs in Opera. The Go menu lists the previously visited URLs in Netscape Navigator.

♦ **View, Go To, URLs.** This command acts like the downward-pointing arrows in the Back and Forward toolbar buttons, opening a list of Web pages you've already visited in this Web session. To jump to a page, click its URL or page title in the list. The Navigation menu includes these commands in Opera. The Go menu includes these commands in Netscape Navigator.

♦ **View, Stop/Refresh.** The Stop and Refresh commands in the View menu perform the same actions as their toolbar counterparts. In both Opera and Netscape Navigator, the command is Reload. It's located in the View menu in Opera and in Netscape Navigator.

♦ **Favorites, Add to Favorites.** If you find a Web page that you'd like to visit repeatedly, click this command to save its location in your Favorites list. The Bookmarks menu is used to store URLs in Netscape Navigator and Opera.

♦ **Favorites, URLs.** When you select the Favorites menu, a list of URLs and/or Web page titles appears; these are Web sites you added yourself, as well as ones that were pre-defined in the browser. To visit one of these sites, click its title in the Favorites menu. To learn more about managing and organizing your Favorites or Bookmarks, please see Chapter 5.

Most Web browsers include numerous other commands that are unique to them or that drive advanced controls that aren't covered in this chapter.

Understanding URLs

To access a Web site and its pages, you must supply an Internet or Web address, known as a URL (Uniform Resource Locator). Here are some sample URLs:

- ✦ http://www.gateway.com

- ✦ http://www.microsoft.com/windowsxp/

- ✦ http://www.yahoo.com

- ✦ http://www.ebay.com

- ✦ http://www.amazon.com

URLs have six parts. However, every URL does not use all of those parts. In fact, most URLs you'll see in print or hear over the radio will only include what's called the domain name, such as "www.gateway.com."

Here's an example of a complete URL with pointers to its various parts:

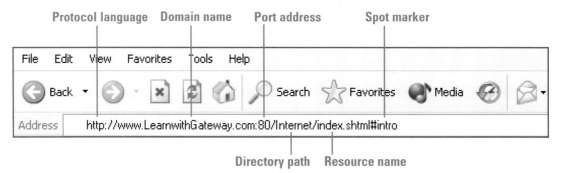

- ✦ **Protocol language.** This indicates the set of rules and standards that allows computers to communicate. For example, http:// refers to the HTTP protocol (HTTP stands for Hypertext Transfer Protocol, the computer language of the Web). This element of a URL is often left out because Web browsers assume HTTP is the default protocol. If, however, the resource is of some other type, such as FTP (File Transfer Protocol), it must be specified, for example, ftp://site.com.

- ✦ **Domain name.** This indicates the IP (Internet Protocol) address of the computer, or where the Web resource is located.

IP addresses actually consist of numbers, such as 216.52.41.129, but the Internet enables users to enter text-based domain names, such as "www.gateway.com", which are then converted to their numerical counterparts. The domain name is the text-based equivalent of the numerical IP address.

✦ **Port address.** Similar to a post office box number; it tells your browser exactly what cubbyhole to request its resource from. Most URLs do not include a port address because HTTP resources use port 80 as their default.

✦ **Directory path.** Lists the subfolders on the Web site or Web page within which a specific resource resides. It's okay for a directory path to include multiple names (representing subfolders within subfolders) such as **/country/promotions/peek**, as long as the domain name or IP address and each folder name is separated by a forward slash (/).

✦ **Resource name.** The actual name of the file containing the Web page or other resource that the URL identifies. In most cases, a resource name is nothing more than a file name. A resource name must be separated from the domain name or IP address or the last folder name by a forward slash (/).

✦ **Spot marker.** Names a specific location within a Web page. Spot markers rarely appear in printed URLs, but they appear often in the Address bar of your browser while you're navigating inside a Web page. Add a spot marker to a URL by adding a number sign (#) followed by a unique name, such as #intro or #footnote. If you type a URL with a spot marker, your browser will load the Web document and then jump or scroll automatically to the exact location named.

 As you're surfing the Web, occasionally glance at the URL listed in the Address bar of your Web browser. The different parts of the URL will change as you move around a Web site or Web page.

 To understand URLs, domains, hyperlinks, and browsers, go to the CD-ROM segment *Navigating the Web*.

Entering Web Addresses

To instruct your Web browser to visit a specific Web address, simply type it in. It's very important to be exact when typing a Web address. If you misspell it or leave out any required element, your Web browser won't go where you want it to.

You can enter a URL into a Web browser in either of the following ways:

◆ Type it directly into the Address field

◆ Type it into a special URL dialog box

To enter a new address directly into the Address field, perform the following steps:

1 Click in the **Address** field.

2 If the current URL is highlighted, press **DELETE** and then skip to step 4.

3 If the current URL is not highlighted, press **HOME**, hold down **SHIFT**, and press **END** to highlight the URL and then press **DELETE**.

4 Type the new URL.

5 Press **ENTER**. In Internet Explorer or Opera, you can click **Go** instead of pressing **ENTER**.

The actions for opening a special URL dialog box are different for each browser:

◆ In Internet Explorer, you can either choose **Open** from the File menu or press **CTRL+O**.

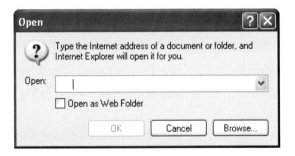

◆ In Netscape Navigator, you can either choose **Open Web Location** from the File menu or press **CTRL+SHIFT+L**.

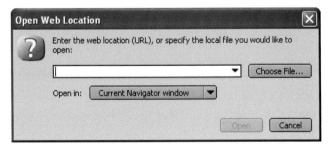

✦ In Opera, you can either choose **Go to page** from the Navigation menu or press **F2**.

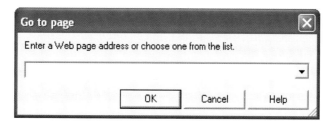

When the URL dialog box opens, type your URL in the text field and then click **OK** or **Open**.

 To practice locating Web pages with the Netscape browser, go to the Web segment *Netscape: Locating Web Pages* in the Netscape course.

Surfing the Web

Surfing is really nothing more than entering URLs manually and clicking hyperlinks to explore various sites. Once a Web page is open and displayed in your Web browser, you're ready to surf. A Web page can be made up of a myriad of images and text sections. Web pages also often include hyperlinks. *Hyperlinks,* or *links,* are text or graphical elements on a Web page that you can click to go to another Web page or resource.

Sometimes it's difficult to visually distinguish hyperlinks from the other elements on a Web page. Text links typically appear in a different color than surrounding text and are underlined. To distinguish images or text that act as links from nonlinked images and text, move your mouse pointer over the element. The pointer changes from an arrow to a hand with a pointing finger when the element is a link.

Anytime your pointer is a hand with a pointing finger, you can click your primary mouse button to activate the link. By activating a link, you tell the Web browser to open and display the resource the link is pointing to.

 In Chapter 5, you'll learn how to search for specific sites or types of information. Understanding how to search for resources adds a whole new dimension to Web surfing.

Encountering Error Messages

As you surf the Web, you're bound to come across Web pages or resources you can't access. When you're unable to access something, the Web browser displays an error message. You'll probably encounter many types of errors as you surf the Web, but missing resources and missing Web servers are the two most common.

 Don't automatically assume that you made a mistake if you receive an error message when surfing the Web. The Web is constantly changing, and many URLs you may come across are out-of-date.

A missing resource message means either the hyperlink or URL pointing to a resource is incorrect or the resource has been moved or deleted. When you encounter this problem, you'll often see an error stating that the resource cannot be found. This type of error is known as a 404 error.

A missing Web server message indicates that the hyperlink or URL pointing to a resource is incorrect, the Web server is not online, or there is no Web server at the specified domain name. When you encounter this problem, you'll often see an error stating that the Web server cannot be reached. This type of error is known as a 500 error.

 Internet Explorer has a default message that pops up but sometimes you'll actually see an error page that says there's a 404 or 500 error. If you ever see either of these errors, you'll know what they mean.

When you encounter an error, try accessing the resource again by performing the following steps:

1 Click **Back**.
2 Click **Reload/Refresh**.
3 Click the hyperlink that failed.

If you still can't access the resource and you're using a dial-up connection, try the following steps:

1. Click your Web browser's Close button (the button with the X in the upper-right corner).
2. Right-click the Internet connection icon in the notification area and then choose Disconnect from the shortcut menu.
3. Click start, click Connect To, and then click your Internet connection.
4. Wait for the Internet connection to be established.
5. Click start and then click Internet.
6. Try to access the resource that failed by typing in its URL or clicking hyperlinks to reach it.

If the resource is still inaccessible, the problem is beyond your control. You can try again later to see if the problem has been discovered and fixed by the people who maintain the site.

Quick Links to the Web

Now that you have Internet access and understand the basics of using a Web browser, you can immerse yourself in the Web. We've put together a tour of many popular and useful Web sites. However, instead of listing that tour here in the book, we've posted it to a Web site. By keeping our URL list on the Web, we can maintain and update that list actively.

 To locate our selection of URLs, check out the table at the end of this chapter.

Go to the CD-ROM and select the segment:

✦ *Navigating the Web* to understand URLs, domains, hyperlinks, and browsers.

✦ *Internet Explorer: Navigating the Web* to see the key features of the Internet Explorer browser.

✦ *Netscape: Navigating the Web* to see the key features of the Netscape Navigator browser.

Go online to **www.LearnwithGateway.com** and log on to select:

✦ *Internet Explorer:: Overview*

✦ *Internet Explorer:: Interface*

✦ *Netscape Introduction*

✦ *Netscape: Locating Web Pages*

✦ *Internet Links and Resources*

✦ *FAQs*

Gateway offers a hands-on training course that covers many of the topics in this chapter. Additional fees may apply. Call **888-852-4821** for enrollment information. If applicable, please have your customer ID and order number ready when you call.

CHAPTER 4

Doing More Online

When the Internet was first created, it was a bare-bones operation, used exclusively for written communication and file transfers. But as more people started going online and commercial use of the Internet was permitted, developers saw a golden opportunity to create technology that allowed people to do more than send messages and files back and forth. They invented special markup languages, such as HTML (Hypertext Markup Language), which allowed individuals to create simple Web pages.

Improvements to imaging technology made it possible for people to scan photographs and send them over the Internet. Faster modems and Internet connections made it possible to send and download data more quickly, paving the way for companies, individuals, and organizations to create massive Web sites containing lots of information—such as pictures, videos, and audio clips—and "open the doors" to the first online shopping environments. Once database connectivity via the Web and other interactive technologies were introduced, it gave people a chance to play games or chat with others online. These and other advances were made at an astonishing pace, and advances continue to be made to this day.

As you start to explore the Internet, you'll want to take advantage of these fascinating features. Connecting your computer to the Internet not only gives you immediate access to astonishing amounts of information, but it also allows you to perform many other activities of daily life with ease. Whether you want to buy a book, find a job, play a game, create a Web-based photo album, or help your kids with their homework, you can do it online. In this chapter, you'll find out how to make the most of the Internet.

Shopping Online

Where there's money to be made, the entrepreneurs won't be far behind. Literally thousands of online retail stores have set up shop over the past five years or so, making shopping one of the most popular activities on the Internet. It's so popular that many brick-and-mortar stores (i.e., those buildings where you can go to shop) are finding that online shopping is creating significant competition. Today you can purchase almost anything—including groceries, clothing, books, housewares, cars, and electronics—online.

People have discovered that they can get what they want online in a fraction of the time it takes to shop in brick-and-mortar stores. They don't have to deal with traffic, crowds, or salespeople; they can have their purchases delivered to their door; and they can do it all while wearing their pajamas! The old saying "shop 'til you drop" doesn't really apply to Internet shopping.

How to Shop

Shopping online is usually a simple process. In most cases, the hardest part is finding the store you want. (We'll talk about finding stores a bit later.) But once you're at an online store, what should you do?

Although each online store has unique features and layout, they almost all have a few common elements:

✦ A catalog or list of their products

✦ A search tool to find products

✦ A virtual shopping cart

✦ A virtual checkout

Figure 4-1 shows Amazon.com®, which is a very well-known online store.

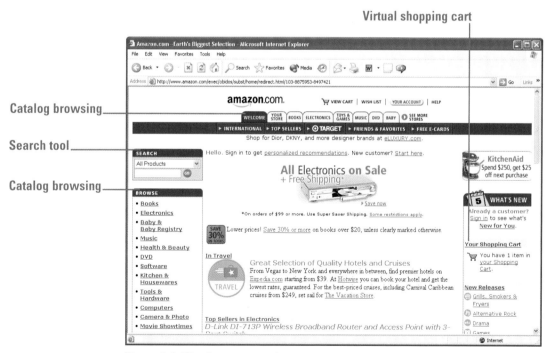

Figure 4-1 The Amazon.com home page.

From the home page of an online store, you usually have two options. You can either browse through its entire inventory or use a search tool to find what you want. If you already know exactly what you want, search tools are usually the best way to go. You only need to type the name of the item, and if the retailer sells it, you'll be quickly taken to it. (See Chapter 5 for more discussion on search tools.)

If you need to look around or "browse" for ideas and get a sense of what the online store is like, check out its online catalog. An *online catalog* is usually a collection of the products sold by the store, with pictures, descriptions, and prices of the items. Online catalogs may be arranged alphabetically, by product code, by manufacturer, by category, by price, or by a myriad of other possible organizational schemes.

 To view an online store's catalog, look for links that include obvious words such as *products, browse, catalog, index, inventory,* and so on.

To navigate within a catalog, either scroll through the site or click the buttons (such as Next, Forward, Previous, Back, etc.) that appear on the virtual pages of the online catalog. On most sites, you can click on images or product names to access more detailed information, including price, product description, whether the product is in stock, and even a bigger picture of the item.

After you find an item you want, there should be a button you can click to order it, add it to a shopping cart, or purchase it (Figure 4-2). On many Web sites, clicking this button will place the item into your virtual shopping cart.

Order item button

Figure 4-2 A product page at Amazon.com.

A *virtual shopping cart* is the Internet equivalent of a shopping cart at the grocery store. As you explore an online store, you place items that you want to purchase into the shopping cart. Most online stores include a link to let you view the contents of your shopping cart at any time (Figure 4-3).

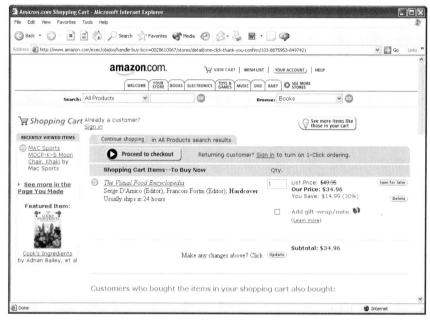

Figure 4-3 A shopping cart at Amazon.com.

Your online shopping cart is similar to shopping carts in traditional stores in that you can't take your shopping cart filled with items you haven't purchased into another store. However, unlike a real store, you do not have to purchase the items in your virtual shopping cart before you leave an online store's Web site—if you change your mind, you can surf the Web and come back later if you decide to purchase the items or put the items back (delete them from your shopping cart).

More About . . . Shopping Carts

A few online stores, such as Amazon.com and Half.com, have very sophisticated shopping carts. In fact, to shop there at all, you have to register with the site. When you register with an online store, you establish a user account. The account keeps track of your purchases, stores multiple shipping addresses, and retains your credit card information if you want it to. A user account makes it easy to see what you've ordered in the past, track shipped orders, and define your likes and dislikes for more focused shopping. Another benefit of having an account at an online store is that, on most sites, you can place an item into your virtual shopping cart and then leave the Web site, and when you return to the site, the items you placed in the virtual shopping cart will still be there.

After you've made your selections and placed your items in your shopping cart, it's time to check out. Just as you can at the grocery store, you go to the checkout counter to pay for the items you want to buy. Some online stores have a link to jump directly to checkout, whereas others may require that you view the contents of your shopping cart before the checkout link is displayed. At checkout, you may perform the following tasks:

- ✦ Fill in your shipping address

- ✦ Select a shipping method

- ✦ Choose whether to gift wrap the products

- ✦ Select a billing method or credit card type

- ✦ Provide your billing address

- ✦ Provide a phone number and/or e-mail address

After you've entered all the requested information, the online store usually asks you to review your order once more and then click a **Submit** or **Confirm** order button to place the order.

Credit Card Safety

Many people won't shop online because they fear *credit card theft,* or the unauthorized use of a credit card to make a purchase. Ironically, more credit card thefts happen in person than online. Yes, there have been well-publicized occurrences of online credit theft, but they are few and far between.

This isn't to say that online credit card theft doesn't take place. Rather, the media heavily publicizes the few thefts that do occur. Making purchases online with a credit card can be more secure than making a purchase at a brick-and-mortar establishment.

 To understand the purpose of digital certificates in Internet Explorer, go to the Web segment *Digital Certificates* in the Internet Explorer course.

Online Security

Online purchases are more secure for several reasons. Reputable online stores use sophisticated security mechanisms to protect your credit card and contact information. (To learn how to determine whether an online store is reputable, see "Choosing a Reputable Online Store" later in this chapter.) Basically, this security mechanism *encrypts,* or encodes, the information sent between your Web browser and the online retailer's Web server. This mechanism is known as *SSL (Secure Sockets Layer),* but how it actually works isn't important. What is important is that SSL-protected Web communications are especially difficult to access. When you submit your credit card information to an online store, your data is sent quickly, so it's unlikely that anyone will be able intercept it, and even if it were intercepted, it would take years to break the security code to extract the contents.

In addition to protecting the communication between your Web browser and their Web servers, reputable online stores also have an encrypted and protected database in which your information is stored. Most stores don't retain your credit card information any longer than necessary to process your order, charge your card, and verify that they have received the money for your purchase. Once that transaction is completed, most online stores delete your credit card information from their database.

 Some online retailers offer the option of storing your credit card information, simplifying the steps you need to take the next time you place an order with them. It's up to you whether to take advantage of this option.

Improve Online Credit Card Security

You can take a few precautionary actions to even further improve the security of your credit cards online.

You can decline the opportunity to store your credit card information with the company for future use. Although these stores usually employ additional security precautions to ensure that their credit card information database is fully protected, if you're at all nervous about storing your information with the company, don't do it. Simply elect not to save your data when the Web site offers.

Online retailers have joined with credit card companies to make Web shopping safer than making purchases in brick-and-mortar stores. Most credit card companies offer online purchase protection. *Online purchase protection* is a benefit that allows you to dispute a charge on your credit card from any online store. If a purchase you didn't make appears on your statement, the credit card company will remove the charge with no hassle.

Here are a few other tips to ensure that you use your credit card wisely when shopping online:

✦ Always choose reputable stores (as explained in the next section).

✦ Keep track of all purchases made with your credit card so you can pinpoint charges on your statement that shouldn't be there.

✦ When in doubt about an online store's security, call the store directly to place an order (most offer their phone numbers on their order page or on their contact page).

 If you have multiple credit cards, you can even designate one to use solely for online purchases.

Choosing a Reputable Online Store

Making your Internet shopping experience a success isn't all about credit card security; it also involves dealing only with online stores that work at satisfying their customers: they ship products promptly, offer high-quality goods, offer no-hassle returns if you're unsatisfied for any reason, and have a designated customer service area on their Web sites. As a cautious customer, you can usually weed out the less-reputable online retailers quickly.

One of the first and best measurements of the quality of an online store is whether you've actually heard of it before. A well-known online store is much more likely to provide quality online purchasing services than an unknown company. If you don't recognize the store, there are still ways for you to determine whether an online store is reputable. Consider the following:

✦ Find out if it has a brick-and-mortar storefront. You can do this by calling its local chamber of commerce and asking. (For example, if the online store's address is listed in Atlanta, GA, call the Atlanta, GA chamber of commerce.)

✦ Look for a statement on its return policy, purchase guarantees or warranties, and customer comments or feedback.

- ✦ Look for a contact phone number for the store and talk to store personnel and get a feel for them. Call and ask how long the store has been in business, if it has a brick-and-mortar storefront, or any other questions you can think of. If you don't like the answers, don't purchase from the company.

- ✦ Contact the Better Business Bureau and ask if there are any complaints about the company.

If you can't find any information about an online store, take your business somewhere else. Most products can be found at many different online stores, so if you don't trust one, keep looking until you find one you do trust.

The Benefits of Shopping Online

We've already discussed one of the major benefits of shopping online: convenience. Not having to fight traffic, wade through crowds, and deal with salespeople are all positive benefits—not to mention trying to squeeze comparison-shopping into an already busy life. Who has time these days to visit three to six stores to price a single item?

A second benefit is price. With a little effort, you can usually find what you want for a substantial discount online. However, it's important to find out what the final in-hand price is. The *final in-hand price* is the amount of money you have to spend to get the product to you. When you make a purchase online, the final in-hand price will include the product's cost minus any discounts or coupons, plus any applicable taxes, packaging or handling fees, and the cost of shipping. Most online stores will allow you to see the final in-hand price before you provide your billing information or at least before you press the final confirm or submit order button. Pay very close attention to the final price, so you can compare true costs from multiple online and brick-and-mortar stores.

By shopping online, you may be able to avoid paying sales tax. If the online store is based outside of your state, you may not have to pay sales tax. This can be a savings of up to 10 percent, depending on the state you live in. As the cost of your item goes up, the dollar amount you can save on sales tax increases as well.

If you do a lot of online shopping or make high-dollar purchases online, you may want to check with your state revenue agency to see what the guidelines are for your state. In some states you have to pay sales tax if the purchase is over a certain dollar amount.

There's no other way to evaluate the prices from multiple stores as quickly and easily as you can online. Just open multiple Web browsers, surf to different stores, fill your virtual shopping carts, proceed to checkout, and look for the final price. Depending on the item, you might want to compare as few as three stores, or as many as a dozen if the product is fairly expensive.

Getting the Most Out of Online Shopping

Always, always, always print your completed order form before you leave an online storefront. Be sure your printout includes the following information:

✦ Store name and Web address

✦ Order number

✦ Items ordered and prices

✦ Shipping method and delivery time

✦ Online store contact phone number or e-mail

If these items don't appear on the printed order form, find them and write them down. Most online stores will send you an e-mail with this information automatically. But if the e-mail fails to arrive, the printout will be your only guaranteed record of the order.

Why is a copy of your final order important? Well, it helps you remember what you ordered, when, and from where. It helps you keep track of the length of time between the order and the arrival of the product. It also gives you all the information you need to contact the online store if there are problems with the delivery.

When placing an online order, always review the final order form to see if any items are out of stock or backordered. Some stores won't ship incomplete orders, and you may end up waiting weeks or months for your items to arrive at your door.

If you're given the option to have an incomplete order shipped, keep in mind that each separately shipped product will cost you more. One box with five items will always cost less to ship than five items in five separate boxes.

When calculating the shipping time for your order, remember that it often takes 24 to 48 hours for your order to actually leave the online store. So if your chosen shipping method indicates three to five days for delivery, add at least two days from the day you ordered it. Then, using this number, count the days on a calendar, remembering to skip Sundays and holidays. If the order fails to arrive by the day after your revised expected date, contact the store—either through its Web site, via e-mail, or by phone—to inquire about your order status.

Delivery delays are not uncommon, especially around the holidays. If you choose to have your items delivered by the U.S. Postal Service, it delivers on Saturday just like any other day. However, if you choose an alternative means, such as UPS or FedEx, you may have to pay an additional fee for Saturday deliveries.

Where to Start Shopping

Figuring out where to start shopping is often the most difficult part of online shopping. Whereas you already know what brick-and-mortar stores sell the kind of music you like, the clothes that fit you best, and the tools you need for home repair, you might not know the online equivalents of these stores. Often your favorite brick-and-mortar store has an online store, too.

Once you learn how to perform searches (discussed in Chapter 5), you'll be able to use your favorite search engine to locate stores that sell exactly what you want. Until then, you can start by going to well-known shopping sites.

To find shopping sites, use a search engine and search for a store name, a product name, or a product description. For more information on where you can access the links to these online stores, see the table at the end of this chapter.

Bidding at Online Auctions

Retailers aren't the only people taking advantage of the Internet to sell goods. Many individuals now sell items over the Internet using online auction sites. If you like spending your Saturdays attending estate, farm, or collectible auctions, you're going to love bidding online.

You've probably already heard of eBay, which is the most well-known online auction site, but there are several others, many of them devoted to specific kinds of items. The great thing about online auctions is that they take place all the time (no need to get up early on Saturday mornings to find the best deals), and you can find thousands upon thousands of items upon which to bid.

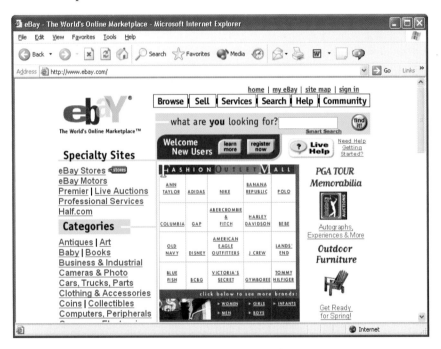

Individuals and companies offer the items you bid on at online auctions. If you're the top bidder when the bidding period expires, you've purchased the product. The bidding period will be clearly posted on the auction site, and you'll be notified via e-mail at the end of the auction if you were the highest bidder.

Started time

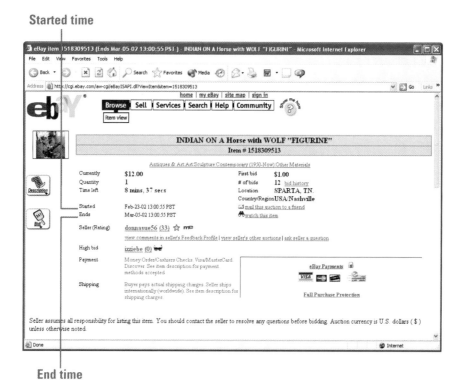

End time

More About . . . Items at Online Auctions

Just as with auctions you travel to, many of the items offered through online auction are usually used, old, antique, damaged, or repaired. If a used product is just as good to you as a brand-new one, auctions can help you find what you want at a discounted price. If an item you're looking for isn't on the market any longer— say, the manufacturer discontinued the item or it's out of stock—auctions may be your only means to obtain it. However, note that some people do sell unused items that are still in the original packaging on auction sites, so you may be able to find some new items.

When you bid on an item, you're effectively entering into a contract with the seller to purchase the product at your bid price. If you're the highest bidder at the end of the auction, you're obligated to purchase the item. Furthermore, if the highest bidder is somehow disqualified and you're the next-highest bidder, you must purchase the item. The only way to get out of the purchase contract is to retract your bid, which is covered later.

The auction communities at eBay and most other online auction sites have extensive checks to ensure that both the bidder and the seller are protected during a transaction. This means that you will be held responsible for paying for an item in an auction that you win and at the same time the seller is held responsible for delivering the product to you as advertised.

Auction Shopping Advice

When trying to compute the final in-hand price of an item purchased through an online auction, keep in mind that shipping and handling costs are determined by the seller. Always find out exactly how much you'll be charged for shipping and handling before you bid. You should also find out if you need to pay sales tax on an item or insure it. If this information isn't included in the item's description, send an e-mail to the seller asking for more information. Clicking on the seller's name will usually open an e-mail dialog box in which you can compose your message.

Auctions can help you discover treasures at an incredible price. But it's also easy to get caught up in the excitement of bidding and get stuck paying too much. In other words, you could end up paying more at auction for an item that you could have purchased from a normal online store for less. It's always a good idea to price shop online before you start bidding in an auction. If you know what you can purchase the item for through a normal online retailer (if it's available), this will help you determine the maximum bid you can enter and not overpay.

Just as with store sites, you can explore auction sites by viewing their catalog of current offerings or searching for a specific item. When searching for a specific item, you can either search using the item's exact name (such as "Ming Tulip Vase") or a concise description (such as "glass vase"). See Chapter 5 for more about searching.

Don't forget to take the time to comparison shop. On any given day, the same auction site may have numerous auctions for the same or similar items. Other auction sites may have auctions for the same item, too. If you can find the item on an auction site that's not as well known, you may have a better chance at getting a lower price. If you can find an item at multiple auctions, you can choose which auction to use based on the item's description or listed additional costs at each auction.

 You should also check out the feedback ratings on the seller. The more positive the rating, the safer the transaction should be. You can typically find the feedback rating clearly marked on the item's page. For example, on eBay, the area in which you can find this information is labeled Seller (Rating).

Placing a Bid

Once you find an item you want to bid on, take the time to carefully read the item's description. You can usually send the seller an e-mail inquiry if you have any questions about the product or any additional fees.

After you're sure you want an item, decide the amount you're willing to spend to purchase the item (i.e., your maximum bid). Once you've determined your maximum bid, place a bid on the item for any amount up to your maximum bid or the highest you'll pay for the item. Although this is called your maximum bid, you can increase the amount of your bid during the transaction.

Even if you win an auction, it doesn't mean that you'll have to pay your maximum bid. Auction sites are designed so that you pay only as much for an item as is necessary to beat the next highest bid and still be below your maximum bid. If someone else bids on an item but bids below your maximum bid, the auction system readjusts your bid automatically to beat the other bidder. To make this clear, let's walk through a possible auction scenario. In this scenario, a seller is auctioning an antique figurine:

1. The seller sets a minimum starting price of $20 and sets the bid increment to $1.

    Sellers can choose to set a minimum starting price, also called a reserve, or leave the bid open, meaning that there's no minimum price. Bid increments are usually set at one-dollar increments, so if the bid on an item is already $20, the next bid would have to be at least $21.

2. Bidder1 places a bid of $25. Because the minimum starting price is $20 and no other bidders have made a bid, the auction remains at $20, with Bidder1 listed as the current top bidder.
3. Bidder2 places a bid of $22. The auction site automatically increases Bidder1's bid to $23 and lists Bidder1 as the current top bidder.
4. You place a bid of $45 (your maximum bid). The auction site automatically increases the current bid to $26 (one dollar more than Bidder1's maximum bid) and lists you as the current top bidder.
5. Bidder1 increases his or her maximum bid to $35. The auction site automatically increases the bid to $36 and lists you as the current top bidder.
6. The bidding time period ends and you win the auction at $36.

To increase your chances of winning the bidding for an item, try waiting until the final moments of the bidding time period to place your bid. Most auctions last 5 to 10 days. If you bid early, other bidders have plenty of time to outbid you. If you bid in the last minute or so of the bidding time period, you don't give other bidders the chance to up the bid.

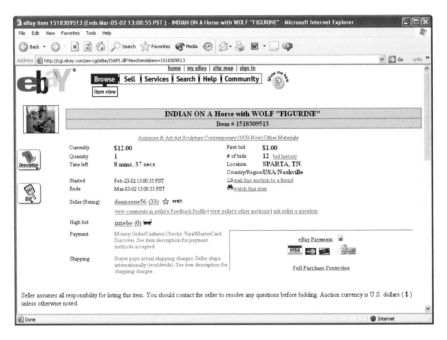

Holding off your bidding until the end of the bidding time period also helps keep the bid frequency low. As the number of bids increases, it may attract even more bidders who are looking for a good deal on a hot item. By waiting until the last minute to place your maximum bid, you'll avoid frenzied overbidding against others.

Retracting a Bid

Everyone who attends auctions knows that they should avoid making any abrupt moves while the bidding is taking place. Accidentally adjust your hat or call a friend at the wrong time and you just might end up buying that bicycle with two flat tires and no seat.

In addition, you have to be careful when entering your bid amount. If you make a mistake and bid incorrectly, such as typing in 10000 instead of 100.00, first try to retract the bid on your own. The process of retracting a bid is usually explained in the help section of the auction site. For exact details and procedures, search on "retract bid" through the auction Web site's help or customer service area. If you're unable to retract the bid on your own, contact the seller immediately and ask for your bid to be retracted.

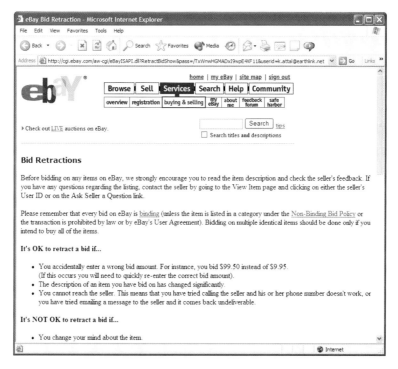

 Auction sites often prevent bidder-controlled bid retractions during the last 24 hours of an auction, so you may not be able to retract a bid without help from the seller.

Winning a Bid

Once you win an auction, you're required by the terms of the auction site's agreement to contact the seller within three days to discuss payment methods and shipping details.

 Most auction Web sites offer a means by which you can pay with a credit card—even to an individual. But some sellers require a money order, a personal check, or an account with an online payment company (such as PayPal and Billpoint, Inc.).

Make sure you print the completed auction item page. That way, you'll have a record of the auction, end date, contact information, and item description. After about 10 days, many auction sites delete completed auctions from their database. So, if you don't make your own printed record of the auction, you may not be able to obtain one later.

 It's a good idea to read the instructions and terms and conditions of an auction site before placing a bid. You'll want to be aware of the requirements, restrictions, and penalties associated with an auction site before participating. The rules and restrictions are designed to protect both the buyer and the seller.

If you ever suspect that you've been cheated or that you've received a product that doesn't match the description, contact the seller immediately. If the seller fails to provide a satisfactory solution, contact the auction site's customer service department and issue a complaint. In most cases in which you can prove fraud, you'll be able to get your money back if you agree to ship the item back to the seller.

 To find auction sites, use a search engine and search on "auctions". For more information on where you can access the links to these auction sites, see the table at the end of this chapter.

Looking for Career Resources

If you need a new job, you'll be happy to know that finding a new job has gotten easier using the Internet. You can now easily access employment ads published in most newspapers across the country. You can submit your resume and letter of application to potential employers via the Internet with the click of a button, saving time, postage, and even gas mileage.

 As a courtesy to their members, many professional organizations have Web pages on which members and others can post jobs.

There have been several career Web sites available since the 1990s to help put potential employers in touch with potential employees. Employers looking to fill positions can post job descriptions to the sites, and job seekers can browse the sites in search of that perfect job. Likewise, people in the job market can post their resumes to the Web sites and apply for posted jobs right online.

Career sites often also include resume writing help, information on continuing education, and tips for improving your interview skills. Some career Web sites offer their services for free, and others charge a fee. Monster®, shown in Figure 4-4, is one of the many career sites.

Figure 4-4 Monster.com home page.

Many features on career Web sites, such as job-hunting tips and career advice, are accessible from their main page. Most of the advanced job search features and capabilities of a career site, however, are available only after you create a personalized user account to store your resume and job preferences. This information helps to ensure that the career information you receive is appropriate for your needs and wants.

Every career site is different, so read the material presented on the site to learn what services are offered and how to look for job opportunities. Many sites offer a tutorial or help section that explains how to use the site.

To find career sites, use a search engine and search on "jobs" or "careers". To find out where you can get more information on career sites, see the table at the end of this chapter.

Sharing Photos Online

Not since the development of the point-and-shoot camera has there been the interest in photography that we're witnessing today, and the Internet has played a huge part in its popularity. Whether you have a digital camera or a traditional film camera and a scanner (or you get your film printed onto photo CDs), you can now send photos to other people through e-mail or upload them to a photo-sharing Web site.

Sending photos through e-mail is as easy as attaching the photo file to the e-mail message before you send it. Please see Chapter 8 for information on e-mail attachments.

Several companies offer digital photo-sharing communities that you can use to share your favorite pictures with friends, family, or the whole world. You can usually define who you want to have access to your photos on these sites, making them ideal online photo albums.

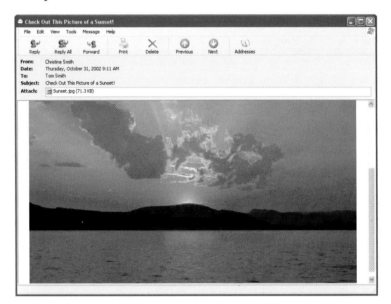

Each online photo sharing service works differently, so read the tutorial and help information to learn exactly how to upload pictures and share them with others using that specific service.

 To find photo sites, use a search engine (see Chapter 5) and search on "Internet photo" or "online photo". To find out where you find more information on photo-sharing services, see the table at the end of this chapter.

Playing Online and Multiplayer Games

One of the most fun interactive activities you can participate in online is to play games with other people, no matter where the players are. You can play backgammon with a complete stranger who lives in Budapest, chess with an old college buddy on the East Coast, and cards with your grandpa in Chicago.

An *online game* is any game you play on the Internet, whether it's a single-player game or involves many people from all over the world. Online games include board games, card games, word games, logic games, traditional-style video games, and fantasy games. Games played between two or more people are called *multiplayer games.*

 Not all online games require more than one person to play, so if you're more interested in practicing your chess techniques or brushing up on your solitaire skills by yourself, you can do that, too.

MSN Zone Games and Windows XP

Windows XP includes several games that you can play against other opponents over the Internet, including Internet Backgammon, Internet Hearts, Internet Checkers, Internet Reversi, and Internet Spades.

To play one of these five games, establish your Internet connection and then launch the game from the Games section of the start menu (click **start**, **All Programs**, and then **Games**). For example, if you want to play Internet Backgammon, perform the following steps once Windows XP is up and running:

❶ Click **start**, point to **All Programs**, point to **Games**, and then click **Internet Backgammon**. The MSN Zone.com Backgammon welcome screen appears.

❷ Click **Play**.

3 The gaming program connects to the gaming server and finds an opponent for you. Once an opponent is found, the backgammon game board appears and the game can begin. To start the game, click **Roll**.

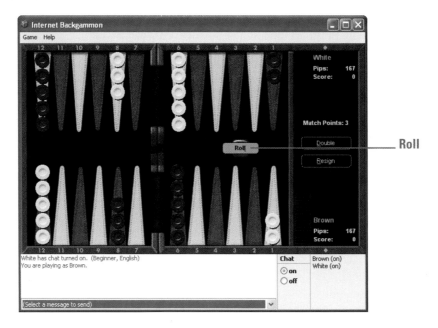

Roll

4 If you need help learning how to play Backgammon or how to control the interface, click the **Help** menu and then click **Backgammon Help Topics**.

   The five games included with Windows XP are just a sampling of the games offered through the MSN Zone.com online gaming service. You can check out any of the hundreds of online games offered through the MSN Zone by accessing the zone.com URL through your Web browser.

Multiplayer Gaming Sites

If you already own stand-alone computer games such as WarCraft III or Rainbow Six: Black Thorn (just to name a couple), you can play those games with other players using the games' multiplayer mode. To play computer games in multiplayer mode, the computers either need to be connected to a network or connected, via the Internet, to a multiplayer gaming site.

   To find gaming sites, use a search engine and search on "online games" or "multiplayer games". To find out where you can find more information on gaming sites, see the table at the end of this chapter.

Every gaming site is different, and the configuration necessary to play a multiplayer game online is also different for each game. Be sure to read the help instructions for your games and the gaming Web site. If you need help, contact the technical support staff for the gaming Web site.

Making the Internet Kid-Friendly

Kids will find lots of games for their age group on the Internet, too. As a matter of fact, the Internet is a great place for kids to do all kinds of things, such as sending e-mail messages to friends and family, doing research for school projects, and getting help with homework. Of course, not all information and activities available on the Internet are appropriate for children. Fortunately, parents can configure many Web browsers, including Internet Explorer, so that their children's experiences on the Internet are positive and fun—and kid-friendly as well.

 To learn about privacy settings and how to create a safer online environment using Internet Explorer, go to the Web segment *Privacy Settings* in the Internet Explorer course.

Creating a Safer Online Environment

Internet Explorer includes several built-in features to help control and restrict the content that can be accessed online. You can use Internet Explorer's Content Advisor to define the type of material to which you want to restrict access. The Content Advisor uses the IRCA (Internet Content Rating Association) internationally recognized ratings to allow or block access to Web sites.

To enable and configure the Content Advisor, perform the following steps:

1. Click **start** and then click **Internet** to open Internet Explorer.
2. Click **Tools** and then click **Internet Options**. The Internet Options dialog box opens.
3. Click the **Content** tab.

4 Click the **Enable** button in the Content Advisor area. The Content Advisor dialog box opens.

5 Click the category you would like to adjust.

6 Select the maximum level of content you wish users of this computer to gain access. Adjust the slider to view the available levels and select the category you want.

7 Click the **Approved Sites** tab.

Type Web
site URL
here

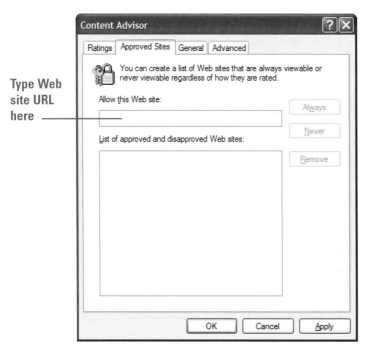

8 If you already know of a specific Web site that you want to grant or prevent access to, type its URL in the Allow this Web site field. If you want users of this computer to access this URL in spite of the Ratings settings, click **Always** (a green circle with a checkmark appears next to the Web site address). If you want users of this computer to not have access to this URL in spite of the Ratings settings, click **Never** (a red circle with a dash in it appears next to the Web site address).

If you have defined a URL that you later want to remove from this tab, select it in the List of approved and disapproved Web sites list box, and then click **Remove**.

⑨ Click the **General** tab.

⑩ If you want to prevent access to Web sites that don't have ICRA ratings, clear the check box named **Users can see sites that have no rating**.

⑪ If you want to allow temporary access to restricted Web sites through parental approval, select the check box named **Supervisor can type a password to allow users to view restricted content**.

⑫ To set the supervisor (or parent) password, click **Create Password**. The Create Supervisor Password dialog box opens. Type a password in both the Password and Confirm password text boxes. You can also type a message in the Hint text field to help you remember this password if you forget it. Click **OK**.

 Windows XP and Internet Explorer are equipped with the ICRA rating system. However, there are other rating systems available. If you purchase or obtain an alternate rating system, it can be installed through the Rating systems button on the General tab of the Content Advisor dialog box. Please see the rating system's own instructions for details on installation and configuration.

⑬ Click **OK** in the Content Advisor dialog box to close it.

If you did not already set a supervisor password (step 12), you'll be prompted to set one before your Content Advisor settings will be applied. Type a password in both the Password and Confirm password text boxes, type a message in the Hint text field if you want to, and click **OK**.

 The Advanced tab of the Content Advisor is not used by the ICRA rating system. It may be used by other systems. If so, details on using that tab will be included in the rating system's user manual.

After you enable Content Advisor, you can always alter your configuration by clicking the **Settings** button on the Content tab. You'll be prompted for the supervisor password before you're allowed to make configuration changes to the Content Advisor. The supervisor password is an important part of the rating control system because it prevents other users from altering the content restrictions.

When a user attempts to access a Web site that is restricted by the settings of the Content Advisor, a dialog box opens. The dialog box states that the Web site is restricted, lists the content ratings (if there are any), and gives you the opportunity to enter the supervisor password to bypass the content restrictions. If you don't enter the supervisor password, click **OK** or **Cancel** to close the dialog box.

If you choose to bypass the content restrictions by providing the supervisor password, you must also select whether to:

✦ Always allow this Web site to be viewed

✦ Always allow this Web page to be viewed

✦ Allow viewing only at this time

If you select either of the first two options, you can always remove the exception by editing the Approved Sites tab of the Content Advisor (see step 8 in the preceding exercise). Once you make a selection and type in the supervisor password, click **OK** to access the Web site.

To completely disable the Content Advisor, do the following:

❶ Click **start** and then click **Internet** to open Internet Explorer.

❷ Click **Tools** and then click **Internet Options**. The Internet Options dialog box opens.

❸ Click the **Content** tab.

❹ Click the **Disable** button in the Content Advisor area. The Supervisor Password Required dialog box opens.

❺ Type the supervisor password and click **OK**. A dialog box opens stating that the Content Advisor has been turned off.

❻ Click **OK**.

❼ Click **OK** to close the Internet Options dialog box.

Kid-Friendly and Family-Oriented Web Sites

You'll be amazed at the creativity and just plain fun you'll find on the many kid-friendly and family-oriented Web sites on the Internet. Your child can take a tour of a virtual museum, watch (and listen to!) a bear hibernate, chat with cartoon characters as well as real people, and the list goes on!

 To find kid and family sites, use a search engine (see Chapter 5) and search on "kid", "children", "youth", or "family". To find out where you can access the links to these kid and family sites, see the table at the end of this chapter.

More About . . . Homework Help

The Web is a fantastic place to find help with homework. Nowadays, teachers may provide you or your child with Web sites to go to for more information on a topic and many schools also have Web-based homework assignments. Contact your child's school to find out if this option is available.

In addition, you can use many of the searching techniques described in Chapter 5 to help you find information on whatever you're studying. The possibilities are endless.

TO KEEP ON LEARNING . . .

 Go online to **www.LearnwithGateway.com** and log on to select:

- ✦ *Internet Explorer: Digital Certificates*
- ✦ *Internet Explorer: Privacy Settings*
- ✦ *Internet Links and Resources*
  - ✦ *Business References*
  - ✦ *Online Stores*
  - ✦ *Online Auctions*
  - ✦ *Online Payment Companies*
  - ✦ *Career Sites*
  - ✦ *Photo-Sharing Services*
  - ✦ *Multiplayer Gaming Sites*
  - ✦ *Kid/Family Sites*
- ✦ *FAQs*

 With the *Survive & Thrive* series, refer to *Create and Share Digital Photos* for more information on:

- ✦ *Working with a digital camera and photo files on your computer*

 Gateway offers a hands-on training course that covers many of the topics in this chapter. Additional fees may apply. Call **888-852-4821** for enrollment information. If applicable, please have your customer ID and order number ready when you call.

Searching the Internet

The Internet is called the information superhighway for a good reason. It quickly puts users in touch with volumes of information. You see, once it became obvious that the Internet was an ideal way to transmit data—including photographs, documents, and Web sites—people wasted no time making the information they wanted the public to have access to available on the Internet. In Chapter 4, you learned about the number of products for sale on the Internet, the games you can play, and the job postings you can view. But that's just the tip of the iceberg.

The contents of entire archives have been uploaded to the Web; university and research libraries have created extensive sites; many magazines and newspapers have digitized their recent and past issues (some going back dozens of years); and the federal government has posted tax documents, laws, and lots of other information to its numerous sites. If you're looking for an answer to a particular question, whether it's about an obscure hobby or a well-known historical incident, there's a very good chance the answer is somewhere on the Internet—all you have to do is find it.

Think of the Internet as a large library, such as the Library of Congress, with thousands and thousands of books. Without the card catalog to help you locate the books that contain information on your subject of interest, you'd have to flip through every book trying to find what you want—not exactly an inspiring proposition. Fortunately, there are tools available to help you search the Internet to locate and identify what you're looking for. In this chapter, you'll find out how to use those tools.

Understanding Search Tools

A *search tool* is a utility on a Web site that searches all or part of the Internet using keywords and other information you supply. A *keyword* is a word that describes the topic you want to search. For example, if you were looking for information on the history of the telephone, an obvious keyword would be *telephone*. If Web sites are found that exactly or closely match your search parameters—the information you asked the search tool to act upon—a list of hits is displayed. A *hit* is a Web page that includes matches for all or part of your search criteria. A hit list is usually displayed with the best possible matches appearing first.

Search Engine vs. Subject Directory

There are two types or classes of search tools. The first type is a search engine, and the second type is a subject directory.

A *search engine* performs its search against Internet content. It uses automated software tools known as spiders, robots, or crawlers to create and maintain a database of information about the Internet. The spiders, robots, or crawlers download nontrivial content from every single Web page they can find on the Internet. Two popular search engines are Google™ and

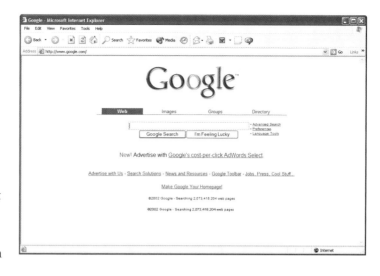

Ask Jeeves®. When you use a search engine to find information, the engine will search its database of information, not live Web sites.

A *subject directory* also performs searches, but instead of searching against the actual content of the Internet as search engines do, it searches against an internal subject catalog (typically separated by categories), which is a database that is maintained on the directory site itself. In most cases, the subject catalog is maintained by people instead of by automated software tools. Yahoo!® is a subject directory.

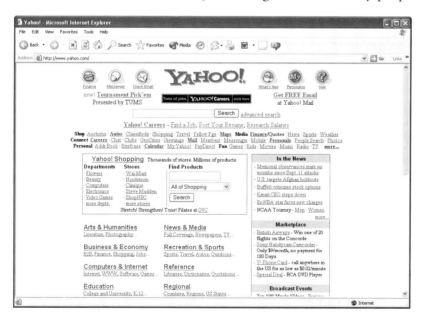

Using a subject directory is almost the same as using a search engine. The differences occur behind the scenes for the most part. The information in search engines is acquired by automated software such as spiders and robots and in subject directories, it's acquired by humans.

However, there are some minor differences when it comes to searching for information. If you need information on a specific item, especially if you know the exact name or title or at least several unique keywords, using a search engine is the best first step. If you need information on a general subject or topic, using a subject directory first will probably be more helpful.

 To learn more about search engines and keywords, go to the CD-ROM segment *Search Engines: Overview.*

Searching for Specific Information Using a Search Engine

Because of the sheer volume of information available on the Web, it can sometimes be a challenge to find the specific information you're looking for. For example, if you're looking for tax forms from the IRS (Internal Revenue Service), simply typing *taxes* into a search engine would return several thousand Web sites. Adding more keywords to your search often helps to limit the number of sites returned by the search engine. You can limit searches in several other ways using *Boolean operators,* which are symbols ($+$, $-$) or words (and, or) that control the inclusion or exclusion of documents in a search. Table 5-1 shows the search symbols used in search engines.

Table 5-1 Search symbols.

SYMBOL	DESCRIPTION	LOCATION	RESULT
+	Plus sign	Between words	Web sites that include both words
−	Minus sign	Between words	Web sites that exclude the word after the minus sign
" "	Quotes	Around a word	Web sites that contain all the words within the quotes as a phrase
and	The word and	Between words	Web sites that contain both words
or	The word or	Between words	Web sites that contain either word

Add the word *and* between two keywords to include both words in a search. Add the word *or* between two keywords to search for either one. Another useful trick is to put your keywords in quotes, which limits the search to the words exactly in the order they appear in the quotes. For example, searching for the words *tax forms* might yield a page from a nonprofit group's site that contains the sentence, "Volunteers should fill out all **forms** before their interview. All donations are considered **tax** deductible." If the keywords are surrounded by quotes, only pages containing both of the words *(tax forms)* in that order will be returned.

You can also modify your search using the + and − signs. Add the + sign in front of a keyword to tell the search engine that the word must be contained in the search results. Adding the − sign in front of a keyword tells the search engine that the word must not appear in search results. This is useful if you're searching for a word commonly associated with other keywords. For example, if you're searching for the history of apple pie, you might want to exclude actual recipes. Therefore, you'd type **apple pie −recipe** in the search engine.

Searching for Specific Information Using a Subject Directory

Some search directories categorize and list Web pages by subject categories. Employees at the subject directory site research the Web pages and place them into appropriate categories. There are pros and cons to this method of searching. On the one hand, it prevents you from getting a lot of miscellaneous search results that just happen to contain your keyword(s). On the other hand, it limits the number of pages included in your

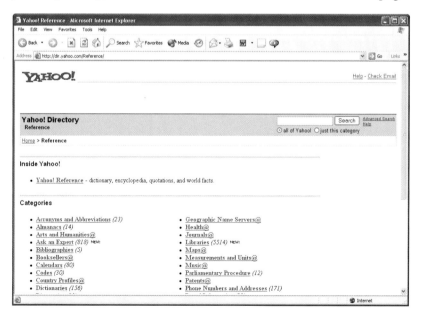

search results to only those that have been placed in the category already. If you try a search through a search engine and your results include an unmanageable number of sites, try using subject directory instead and searching by subject category.

If you're looking for a particular organization's Web site, it never hurts to just type **www.**, the company's name, and the appropriate extension (such as .com, .org, or .gov) into your Web browser's Address bar. Many companies and organizations try to keep their Web address as closely related to their actual name as possible. For example, the IRS home page URL is **www.irs.gov**.

Defining Effective Search Techniques

Let's take a moment to review some effective search techniques that you can use in both search engines and subject directories. Because the search utilities are able to seek out information on a worldwide basis, the number of sites related to the initial search query can be huge. Not all sites included in the search results may be relevant to your topic—most of them probably won't be.

Search engines and subject directories list those search results that are likely to be most relevant to your search at the top of the hit list.

Well-defined search requests help the search engine provide a focused list. For example, if you want to learn about the hibernation practices of black bears, a search on the word *bears* would return hundreds of hits that aren't relevant to your topic, including hits about sports teams, such as the Chicago Bears!

Deploying any of the following search strategies helps refine your search:

✦ Use more than one keyword to make the search as specific as possible; for example, black bear hibernation.

✦ Use a plus sign (+) between the three keywords to limit the search results to those Web sites that include all three words; for example, black+bear+ hibernation.

✦ Place the string of words, or phrase, within quotes; for example, "black bear hibernation" or "hibernation of the black bear".

✦ If the results don't provide you with the information you're seeking, change the order of your keywords or change your keywords.

✦ Use a thesaurus to alter your keywords.

✦ Be as specific as possible.

✦ Avoid common and trivial words such as *and, the, it, is, a, with,* and so on (unless you're using *and* or *or* as Boolean operators).

Using a Search Engine

Now that you know how to search for the information you want, it's time to practice. This exercise uses Internet Explorer on a Windows XP system so if you're running a different version of Internet Explorer, a different operating system, or a different browser, your steps may differ slightly. Try the following exercise to make sure you understand the search techniques we just covered:

1. Make sure you're connected to the Internet.
2. Click **start** and then click **Internet** to open your Web browser.
3. Click in the **Address** field.
4. If the URL in the Address field isn't highlighted, press **DELETE** or **BACKSPACE** to clear any existing URL from the Address field.
5. Type **www.google.com** and then press **ENTER**.
6. The Google search engine's front page appears. Your pointer should already be in the search box above the Google Search and I'm Feeling Lucky buttons. If it's not, click in the search box to place your pointer there.

7. Type a set of keywords to search for, such as **Gateway computers**.

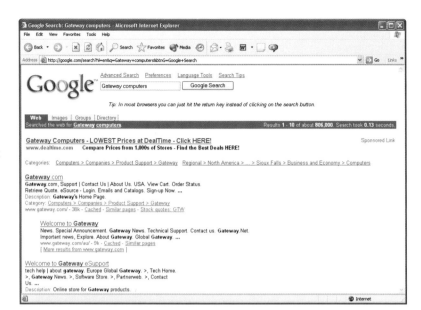

8 Click the **Google Search** button. A list of hits appears.

The search engine interface typically includes ads for Web sites that have paid for advertising space. If you see links that are highlighted or otherwise marked as advertisements, featured sites, or sponsors, keep in mind that they aren't necessarily related to your keyword search.

9 Click the first hit (it appears just below the line that begins with *Categories*), which is a link to the page that best matches your search string. The page opens in your browser.

⑩ Click the **Back** button in the Web browser.

⑪ The list of hits from the search engine appears again. Click the second hit, which is a link to the page that is the second-best match for your search string. The page opens in your browser.

⑫ Click the **Back** button in the Web browser.

⑬ Click the **Back** button in the Web browser again.

⑭ Select the existing text in the keyword text field and replace it by typing **personal computers**.

5

⑮ Click **Google Search**. A new list of hits appears.

As you can see, searching for information involves providing keywords, performing the search, and then visiting the top matches from the search engine. If you don't find what you want, change the keywords or the way they're entered and search again. Once you're finished using the search engine and any Web sites you've found, close your Web browser if you're done using the Internet.

Using a Subject Directory

Using a subject directory is much like using a search engine. To learn how to use a subject directory, try the following exercise:

❶ Make sure you're connected to the Internet.

❷ Click **start** and then click **Internet** to open your Web browser.

❸ Click in the **Address** field.

❹ If the URL in the Address field isn't highlighted, press **DELETE** or **BACKSPACE** to clear any existing URL from the Address field.

❺ Type **www.yahoo.com** and press **ENTER**. The Yahoo! subject directory's front page appears.

❻ Click in the keyword text field to the left of the Search button to place your insertion point.

❼ Type a set of keywords to search for, such as **Gateway computers**.

8 Click **Search**. A list of hits appears. Notice that there are at least two sections relevant to your keyword search. The Category Matches section lists the categories that match your keywords and the Web Site Matches section lists the cataloged Web sites that match your keywords.

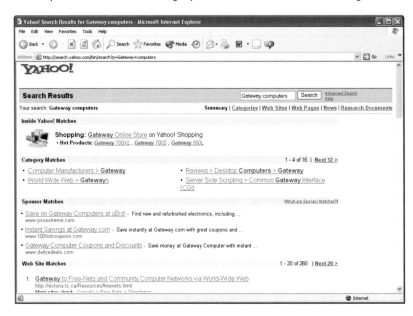

 Just as with search engines, subject directories display ads for Web sites that have paid for advertising space. If you see links that are highlighted or otherwise marked as advertisements, featured sites, or sponsors, keep in mind that they aren't necessarily related to your keyword search.

9 Click on the first category match (it appears just below the line that reads Category Matches). The selected category match information page opens.

10 Click the **Back** button in the Web browser.

11 Click on the first hit (it appears just below the line that reads Web Site Matches). The page that best matches your search criteria opens in your browser.

⑫ Click the **Back** button in the Web browser. The list of hits from the subject directory appears again.

⑬ Click the second hit. The second-best match found by the subject directory opens in your browser.

⑭ Click the **Back** button in the Web browser.

⑮ Click the **Back** button in the Web browser again.

⑯ Type **personal computers** in the keyword text field.

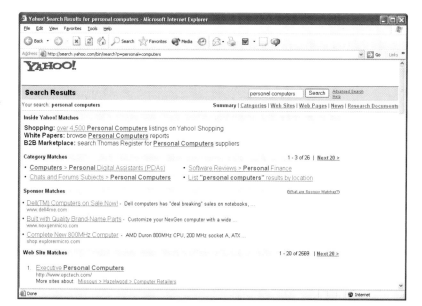

⑰ Click **Search**. A new list of hits appears.

If you don't find what you want, change the keywords and search again. Once you're finished using the subject directory and any Web sites you've found, close your Web browser if you're done using the Internet.

Saving Internet Information

Let's say you've just spent 20 minutes searching for information on the hibernation of black bears. Fortunately, you hit the jackpot: a great site that includes a lot of information about, as well as photographs of, black bear hibernation practices. Of course, you don't want to go through the entire search process the next time you want to visit the site. Fortunately, you can save a lot of time by recording the URL of the site—and any other site you think you'll want to visit again—in a quick-access list (see Chapter 3 for more on URLs). Once it's saved on the list, you only need to click your mouse twice to return to a page that may have taken several searches to discover.

The URLs you store are called different names depending on which Web browser you're using. Internet Explorer calls them Favorites, and Netscape Navigator and Opera call them Bookmarks. No matter what they're called, being able to record the URLs of Web sites in a quick-access list is extremely useful.

 To gain practice saving a Web page with Internet Explorer, go to the Web segment *Internet Explorer: Saving a Displayed Web Page* in the Internet Explorer course.

To explore other ways to save information using Internet Explorer, go to the Web segment *Internet Explorer: Other Saving Options* in the Internet Explorer course.

To practice saving Web pages with the Netscape browser, go to the Web segment *Netscape: Saving Web Pages* in the Netscape course.

Favorites or Bookmarks are stored as elements in a menu of the Web browser. Accessing a stored URL is as simple as clicking the Favorites or Bookmarks menu and locating and selecting a stored Web site's name. The stored URL menu can employ multiple sublevels or folders, just like the start menu. Sublevels or folders make categorizing, grouping, and organizing your favorite Web sites easy.

 Web browsers typically come with some preexisting stored URLs. Some of them may be of interest to you, whereas others may serve only as advertisements for products or services you're not interested in. You can manage (that is, delete and reorganize) the preexisting URLs just as you can your own.

Marking a Favorite or Bookmark

Creating a Favorite or a Bookmark is easy; just perform the following steps:

1 Access the Web site that you want to add to your URL list.

2 Choose the appropriate command for your Web browser:

✦ In Internet Explorer, choose the **Add to Favorites** command from the Favorites menu.

✦ In Netscape Navigator, choose the **Add Bookmark** command from the Bookmarks menu.

✦ In Opera, choose the **Add page here** command from the Bookmarks menu.

3 A dialog box opens and shows the default title and URL for the Web site to be added as a Favorite or Bookmark. Edit the title or accept the existing title.

4 A Web site's URL can be stored in the top level, or main section, of the Favorites or Bookmarks list or in a folder within the list. The URL is automatically stored in the top level unless you select a folder. In Internet Explorer, click the **Create in** button in the Add Favorite dialog box to reveal the existing folder hierarchy.

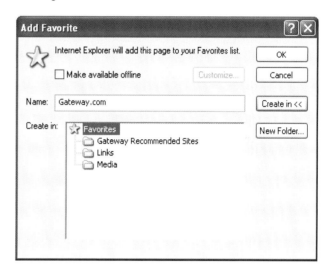

5 Click **OK** to complete the Favorite/Bookmark creation process.

Once a Web site's URL is added to your list, you can access it by clicking the Favorites or Bookmarks menu and clicking the Web site's name.

To see how to save favorite Web pages with the Internet Explorer browser, go to the CD-ROM segment *Internet Explorer Favorites: Adding Web Pages.*

To see how to bookmark Web pages with the Netscape browser, go to the CD-ROM segment *Netscape Bookmarks: Adding Web Pages.*

Editing Favorites and Bookmarks

Once you've added several URLs to your Favorites/Bookmarks, you may want to organize your stored sites into groups. For example, if you've saved the URLs of several sites on the hibernation practice of bears, your two favorite search engines, and all of the home pages for companies in which you own stock, your Favorites or Bookmarks menu could probably use a little organization. You can create three separate folders and name them "Black Bear Hibernation," "Search Engines," and "My Stocks."

Managing the organization of stored URLs involves deleting any unwanted URLs, moving URLs to a folder, renaming URLs and folders, and creating or deleting folders. The actual commands you use to manage the organization of stored URLs are different for every browser, but the general process is the same in each.

If you use Internet Explorer, you can learn how to manage and organize your URLs by performing the following exercise:

1. Make sure you're connected to the Internet.
2. Click **start** and then click **Internet** to open your Web browser.
3. Click in the **Address** field.
4. If the URL in the Address field isn't highlighted, press **DELETE** or **BACKSPACE** to clear any existing URL from the Address field.
5. Type **www.yahoo.com** and press **ENTER**. The Yahoo! subject directory's front page opens.
6. Click the **Favorites** menu and then click **Add to Favorites**. The Add Favorite dialog box opens.

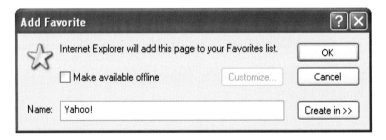

7. Click **OK** to add the Favorite with the default or suggested name.
8. Click the **Favorites** menu. Notice that the Web site you just added appears at the bottom of the list of stored URLs.
9. Click **Organize Favorites**. The Organize Favorites dialog box opens.

⑩ Click **Create Folder**.

⑪ Type the name for the new folder, for example, **Search engines**.

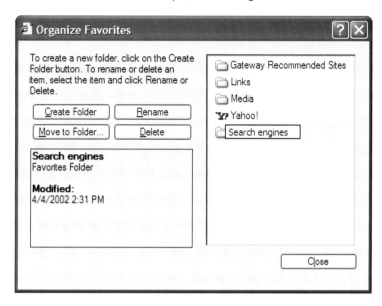

⑫ Press **ENTER**. Click the name of the Yahoo Web site you added back in step 7.

⑬ Click **Move to Folder**. The Browse for Folder dialog box opens. Click the folder you created in step 11 (Search engines).

⑭ Click **OK** and click **Close**.

⑮ Close Internet Explorer and reopen it.

You don't have to close Internet Explorer to see that the site has been added to your Favorites menu. We just ask you to do this so you can open the page. If you don't close Internet Explorer, the page is still open in your browser window.

16 Click the **Favorites** menu, position your mouse pointer over the folder you named in step 11, and click on the Web site name (Yahoo!). Notice that the Web site opens in your browser.

Using this procedure, you can organize hundreds or thousands of your favorite stored Web site URLs. Plus, because you can create folders within folders, there's no limit to the organizational possibilities.

 To practice organizing favorite Web pages in Internet Explorer, go to the Web segment *Internet Explorer Favorites: Organizing* in the Internet Explorer course.

Sending a Link

If you want to share a Web site with a friend, you can e-mail a URL or the Web page itself right from your Web browser. Your computer must be configured to use e-mail (see Chapter 8) before you can e-mail URLs or Web pages from your Web browser.

To send a URL or a Web page to someone via e-mail, perform the following steps:

1 Open Internet Explorer.

2 Access the Web page you want to send.

3 Click the **File** menu, choose **Send**, and then choose **Page by E-mail** or **Link by E-mail**. The Page by E-mail command sends the actual Web page itself to someone as it appears right then and there. The Link by E-mail command sends just the URL of the Web page to someone. In both cases, the element is sent as an attachment to your message.

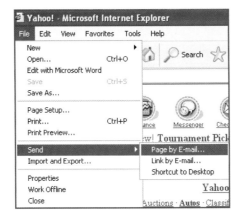

Because of problems with viruses, some e-mail systems will block URLs attached to e-mail messages.

❹ An e-mail message window opens. Type the e-mail address of the intended recipient and click **Send**.

If you don't want to send a Web page as an e-mail attachment but you want to send someone the URL for a Web page in the body of the e-mail, you can do that, too. When you're viewing the Web page in your Web browser, select all of the text in the Address field and then press **CTRL** and **C** at the same time. The CTRL+C keystroke copies the selected text to memory (into a special location called the Clipboard). When you're creating the e-mail message, position your mouse pointer where you want the URL to appear and press **CTRL+V**. The CTRL+V keystroke pastes the contents of the Clipboard to the location of the mouse pointer.

5

 Alternatively, you can select the URL in the Address field, and click **Edit** and then choose **Copy**. Then, compose your e-mail, position your pointer in the body of the message, click **Edit**, and then choose **Paste**.

Printing from the Internet

Another way you can keep track of URLs or create a permanent record of a Web site is to print the Web page. If your computer has a printer attached and properly configured, you only need to click the Print button on the toolbar to print the Web page.

 Some Web sites have what are called printer-friendly versions. They are unique versions of the Web page designed to fit on a regular page when printed. Usually, the Web site will clearly mark a link for the printer-friendly version of that page.

If you want to modify the print parameters, such as the number of pages and the position of the paper, choose the **Print** command from the File menu to open the Print dialog box. The Print dialog box of a browser functions the same way the Print dialog box from the Windows WordPad application functions. When a Web page is printed, the URL and the date are automatically included in the footer of the printed document.

 To be able to print Web pages and to practice setting different page options and previewing pages using Internet Explorer, go to the Web segments *Printing Web Pages* and *Page Options: Settings* in the Internet Explorer course.

To practice printing Web pages using the Netscape browser, go to the Web segment *Netscape: Printing Web Pages* in the Netscape course.

TO KEEP ON LEARNING . . .

Go to the CD-ROM and select the segment:

◆ *Search Engines Overview* to learn more about search engines and keywords.

◆ *Internet Explorer Favorites: Adding Web Pages* to see how to save favorite Web pages with the Internet Explorer browser.

◆ *Netscape Bookmarks: Adding Web Pages* to see how to bookmark Web pages with the Netscape browser.

Go online to **www.LearnwithGateway.com** and log on to select:

◆ *Internet Explorer*

◆ *Netscape*

◆ *Internet Links and Resources*

◆ *FAQs*

Gateway offers a hands-on training course that covers many of the topics in this chapter. Additional fees may apply. Call **888-852-4821** for enrollment information. If applicable, please have your customer ID and order number ready when you call.

Downloading from the Internet

According to Benjamin Franklin, there are only two things we can be certain about in life: death and taxes. The Internet can't do much about the first certainty, but it's taken great strides in making the second—paying taxes—a lot easier. You've probably already heard about e-filing; instead of sending your completed tax forms and check to Uncle Sam via the U.S. Postal Service, you handle the entire transaction over the Internet. No more 11th-hour trips to the post office on April 15th, no more multiple photocopies, and no more worrying about whether you have enough postage on the envelope.

For the average American with Internet access, the Internet has taken at least some of the sting out of tax time by making tax documents—the forms and instructions we all need to file our taxes—available online. Instead of the annual scramble to the library or post office to locate 1040s and other necessary forms (many of which have all been taken by the time you get there, anyway), it's now possible to simply log on to the IRS's Web site to get the tax forms and instructions you need.

And tax forms are only one of millions of items you can transfer from the Web to your computer. It's possible to save documents of all kinds—as well as programs, graphics, music, and even short movies—to your computer. In this chapter, we'll tell you what you need to know to download files from the Internet. After all, April 15th will be here again before you know it.

Downloading and the Internet

The process of copying material from the Internet to your computer is called *downloading*. You can download files from two different kinds of sites: Web sites and FTP sites. You're already familiar with Web sites—they can contain text and graphics, both of which you can download to your computer. FTP sites are text-only sites—they don't contain any images. Web sites are by far the most common kind of site on the Internet today, although you'll occasionally encounter FTP sites as you surf the Web.

 Web sites use HTTP (Hypertext Transfer Protocol) to transfer information, whereas file-sharing sites use FTP (File Transfer Protocol).

Internet Explorer, as well as most other Web browsers, can access both Web and FTP sites, so the distinctions between the two don't really matter. Basically, if you can get to it by surfing through your Web browser, you'll be able to download files.

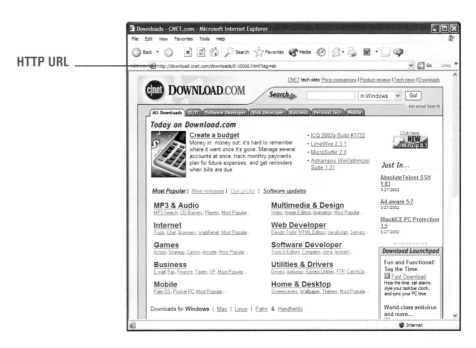

HTTP URL

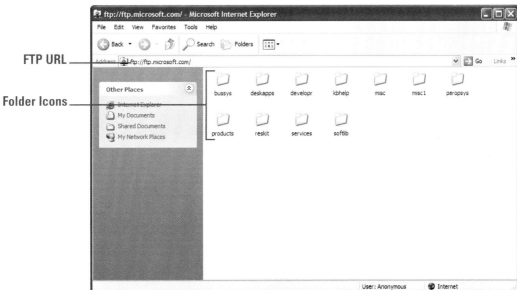

FTP URL

Folder Icons

Some Web and FTP sites require user names and passwords before you can download files, and others allow anonymous access to anyone. Those sites that are protected or secured will prompt you for a valid user name and password. If you don't have a valid user name and password for the site, you'll be unable to access the files stored there.

If you're performing file uploads and downloads constantly on an FTP site, you may want to use a dedicated FTP tool, also sometimes called an *FTP client*. These tools offer more features than your standard Web browser, such as scheduling, synchronizing, and queuing. There are many FTP tools available, including WS_FTP from Ipswitch and CuteFTP from GlobalSCAPE.

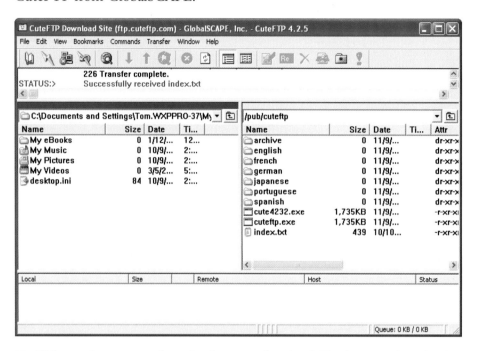

You'll learn the steps to download various kinds of files later in this chapter. First, it's important that you know about the kinds of files you can download, how to open them, and how to protect yourself from computer viruses.

Understanding File Types

Internet sites can contain many different types of files. You can tell what type a file is by its extension. A *file extension* is made up of the characters after the period in a file name. Extensions are usually three characters long, but they can be as short as two characters or as long as four characters or more. There are many types of extensions. Some are used often and by many programs, whereas others are used rarely or only by a specific program. Some of the more common extensions are listed in Table 6-1.

Table 6-1 Common file extensions.

EXTENSION	FILE TYPE	DESCRIPTION	ASSOCIATED PROGRAM(S)
.avi	Movie/video files	Audio Video Interleaved or Video for Windows	Media players
.bmp	Image files	Bitmap graphic	Paint, Web browsers
.doc	Document files	Microsoft Word document	Microsoft Word, WordPad
.exe	Compressed or program files	Self-extracting compressed file or program executable file	Itself, WinZip®
.gif	Image files	Graphics Interchange Format	Web browsers
.htm, .html	Web document files	Hypertext Markup Language file	Web browsers
.jpeg, .jpg	Image files	Joint Photographic Experts Group	Web browsers
.mov, .qt	Movie/video files	QuickTime® Movie	QuickTime Movie Player
.mp3	Music/audio files	MPEG layer 3 audio file	Media players
.mpg, .mpeg	Movie/video files	MPEG movie file	Media players
.pdf	Document files	Portable Document Format	Adobe® Acrobat®
.rtf	Document files	Rich Text Format	Microsoft Word, WordPad
.swf	Movie/video files	Shockwave, Flash	Macromedia Flash player
.tif, .tiff	Image files	Tagged Image File Format	Web browsers
.txt	Document files	Text file	Notepad
.wma	Music/audio files	Windows Media Audio	Windows Media Player
.wmv	Movie/video files	Windows Media Video	Windows Media Player
.zip	Compressed files	Zip archive	WinZip

6

More About . . . Windows XP and Extensions

By default, Windows XP hides the file extensions of files on your computer. Thus, when you view files through My Computer or Windows Explorer, you see the icon associated with the file and the file name without the extension. If you want to view the extensions, you need to disable the hide extension feature. To do so, follow these steps

1 Open My Computer or Windows Explorer.

2 Click the **Tools** menu and then click **Folder Options**.

3 The Folder Options dialog box opens. Select the **View** tab.

4 Scroll down. Clear the **Hide extensions for known file types** check box.

5 Click **OK** to close the Folder Options dialog box.

If you don't have a player or viewer for the type of file you download, you'll be unable to open (that is, access the contents) the file. Fortunately, Windows XP already includes programs that open or play the most common file formats (primarily WordPad, Internet Explorer, and Windows Media Player). However, if you want to access PDF documents and MOV movies, both of which are widely found on Web sites, you'll need to download Adobe Acrobat and QuickTime, respectively.

File Compression and Archiving

Some particularly large files, including many software programs and high-resolution images, may take a while to download with even the fastest Internet connections. With slower modem connections, they can take several minutes or even hours to download. Fortunately, files can usually be compressed, meaning that they're made smaller for transferring over the Internet.

Files that have a .zip, .arj, or .rar file extension are compressed files (also known as *archived files*). When a file is compressed, the size of the data is reduced. Compressed files download more quickly than uncompressed files and take up less disk space. Once you download the file, you can use an archive or compression utility, such as WinZip, to expand the file back to its original size; this process is called *extracting*. The extracted file is an exact copy of the original file before it was compressed.

Some archives, such as that shown in Figure 6-1, can be converted into self-extracting archives. These files have the .exe extension. You don't need any special tools or readers to open a self-extracting archive. All you need to do is open the file by double-clicking its icon. In most cases, a dialog box opens and asks for a destination directory. Once you indicate the location for the extracted file, the self-extraction process will proceed.

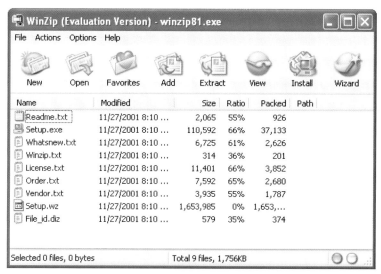

Figure 6-1 The WinZip tool displaying the contents of its own installation file, which is a self-extracting compressed archive file.

A compressed, or archived file, can contain many files and retain their directory structure. For example, you can compress three folders containing several files each into a single archived file and send it over the Internet. When the person you send it to opens the file using an archive utility, he or she will find the three folders and their files intact.

In addition to containing multiple files, a single archive can be split into multiple parts. When an archive file is split, it's divided into individual files that are smaller than 1.44 MB. This allows you to save a very large archive to multiple floppy disks. A split archive can be sent to someone via e-mail by attaching each part to a separate e-mail message.

The size at which you should compress a file varies depending on your Internet connection speed. For fast Internet connections, such as cable modems and DSL lines, you should compress a file when it's approximately 2 MB. For slower connections, such as a dial-up modems, you should compress at 500 KB. Although most text files will be much smaller than this, graphics and music files can be quite large and may need to be compressed, especially if you're sending several at a time.

 Some file types will compress more than others. It all depends on how dense the file format is to begin with. For example, TIF graphic files can compress to about 1 percent of their original size, whereas JPG graphic files might compress to only 80 percent of their original size.

Windows XP gives you the ability to view and extract the contents of ZIP archives (files with the .zip extension). When a ZIP file is on your hard drive, Windows XP automatically treats it like a compressed folder. To view the file's contents, just navigate to the file using My Computer or Windows Explorer.

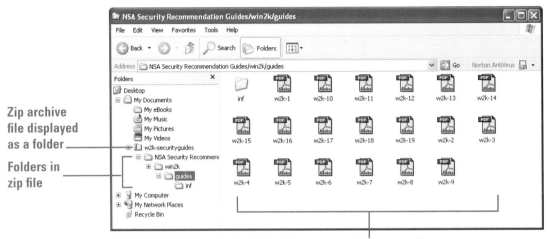

Zip archive file displayed as a folder

Folders in zip file

Files within the zip file

To extract files from the archive, select the archive file and then choose the **Extract All** command from the File menu or right-click and choose it from the shortcut menu.

There are many zip (or archive) tools, but WinZip seems to be the most versatile because it supports a wide range of archive formats, including .arj and .rar plus many others you usually won't run across (such as .arc, .lha, .tar, .z, .gz, .taz, .tgz, etc.).

To find an extraction tool meant specifically for a particular archive format, see the table at the end of this chapter.

Protecting against Viruses

Just like and you and I, computers are susceptible to viruses. A computer *virus* is a small program that attaches itself to files and spreads when a file is copied. Viruses can prevent your computer from working properly and can do serious damage to it. Viruses work in many different ways; from simply replicating themselves, to deleting files or preventing important system functions from working properly.

Viruses can infect program files, document files, image files, music files, system files, and e-mail attachments. Your computer can contract a virus when you open infected files, open e-mail attachments, or even download something from a Web site. It's important to be very careful when you download files so that you don't accidentally download viruses with the files.

A *Trojan horse* is another kind of computer "infection" that can damage your computer. Like the Trojan horse of Greek tragedy, computer Trojan horses are gifts that contain not-so-pleasant surprises. They masquerade as free software or shareware. When you run the Trojan horse, it may perform the task it claims to perform, but it also performs some sort of misdeed as well, such as deleting important files.

An example of a Trojan horse is a program that formats your hard disk by surprise. When your hard drive is formatted, all your personal files and settings are deleted. In some cases, even the operating system, such as Windows XP, is deleted, which makes the computer completely inoperative.

To protect your computer from virus infections and Trojan horse attacks, it's important to take two actions. First, develop *safe surfing* habits. Second, install *anti-virus software*.

Safe Surfing

Safe surfing habits will help keep your computer safe from viruses because you'll avoid places where you're most at risk of getting them. Here are a few guidelines you might want to adopt when looking at Web sites, downloading files, and opening attachments to e-mails:

+ Never download files from questionable sites. A questionable site is one run by an individual or a company that is not well known. If you don't trust a site completely, don't download from it.

+ Use trusted and popular file download repository sites, which offer 100-percent virus-free downloads.

+ If you receive an e-mail attachment from someone you don't know, don't open it. (Details about protecting yourself from potentially harmful e-mail attachments are discussed in Chapter 8.)

+ Avoid Web sites that offer warez (pirated software, viruses, game cheats, and more), cracks (illicit passcodes) or serial numbers for software, adult material, or other illegal items.

 To learn more about security and system protection, go to the CD-ROM segment *Security: Risks and Solutions.*

Anti-virus Software

No matter how vigilant you are about maintaining safe surfing habits, you should still use anti-virus software. Anti-virus software works in the background on your computer, automatically checking for viruses by scanning your e-mail attachments and files you have downloaded from the Web. If it finds any viruses, it removes them before they can do any harm. It can also actively monitor your computer's memory and scan all downloaded files and incoming e-mail messages to stop virus infections before they occur.

Many good anti-virus software packages are available, including Symantec® The Norton AntiVirus®, McAfee VirusScan®, and TrendMicro's PC-cillin®. No matter which tool you select, keep the following important issues in mind:

✦ Because new viruses are created daily, and because the anti-virus software companies must continually find ways to keep viruses from spreading, it's important to download and install updates for viruses regularly. Most anti-virus programs can do this automatically. It's usually sufficient to download updates every two weeks, except when harmful infections become news.

✦ To avoid infection from downloaded files, e-mail messages, and other incoming data, it's essential that you configure anti-virus software to scan your memory and all incoming data automatically. Also, it's a good idea to configure your anti-virus software to scan every file on your computer regularly. In most cases, a once-a-week scan is sufficient.

✦ The anti-virus software you choose must support your operating system; otherwise, the anti-virus software won't work properly.

6

Because every anti-virus software tool is different, we can't provide you with a step-by-step guide to installing and using all of them. Most of these products include a general virus scan capability that you can run from the main program window or as a menu selection. Likewise, most products ask you if they should quarantine or delete any infected items they encounter. When you choose the quarantine option, the infected file is saved to a special directory on your computer; deleting gets rid of the file completely—the latter is the safest option. Most anti-virus products include excellent instructions, so it should be easy to install and configure them on your own.

 If you get stuck, don't hesitate to call the vendor's support line or contact the company that sold you your computer.

Many computers are currently shipped with anti-virus software installed. One of the more common anti-virus programs you'll find installed on systems is Norton AntiVirus. We use it as an example to get you familiar with scanning your computer for viruses.

If Norton AntiVirus is on your computer, you'll see the Norton AntiVirus folder in the All Programs section of the start menu and the Norton AntiVirus Auto-Protect icon in the notification area (assuming it's not hidden).

If you ever suspect you have downloaded or otherwise been infected by a virus, immediately perform a system-wide scan of your computer. To initiate a virus scan of your computer using Norton AntiVirus, perform the following steps:

❶ Click **start**, point to **All Programs**, point to **Norton AntiVirus**, and then click **Norton AntiVirus 2002**.

❷ The Norton AntiVirus window opens. Click **Scan for Viruses**.

❸ The Scan for Viruses screen appears. Click to select **Scan my computer** and then click **Scan**.

❹ The Scan Progress screen appears. As Norton scans your entire computer for viruses, you can watch this screen for progress reports. If any viruses are found, Norton attempts to automatically remove them and repair the infected files.

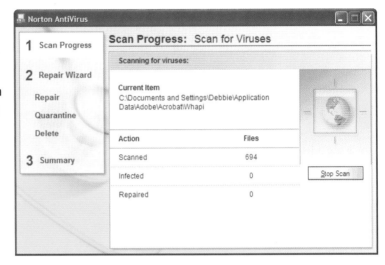

❺ During the course of the scan, if Norton discovers any viruses that it cannot automatically remove, you're prompted to attempt the repair again, move the infected file to a quarantine area, or delete the infected file. In most cases, try the repair again. If the repair fails again, select the **Quarantine** option.

 Norton creates a quarantine folder to which it moves all virus-infected files it's unable to repair. All files within the quarantine area are locked down so they can't be read or opened. This prevents the virus from spreading and also gives you the opportunity to perform other repair actions and possibly recover the file.

⑥ After the scan is complete, a summary report appears. You can view more details about the scan by clicking **More Details**. If you're finished using the Norton AntiVirus utility, click **Finished** and then click the **Close** button (the X in the upper-right corner).

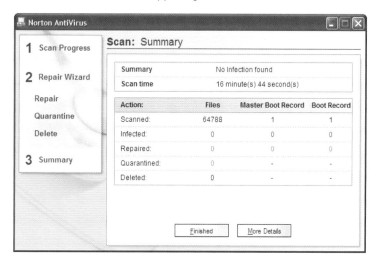

If the scan summary indicates that viruses were found and Norton was unable to remove them, you should contact Norton's technical support for further help. Depending on what virus is discovered and which files are infected, there are many possible solutions to disinfect your computer. For details on obtaining technical support, please see Chapter 14.

 To learn more about how to avoid getting viruses from downloaded Internet files, go to the CD-ROM segment *Anti-Virus Software*.

Downloading Files

Now that you're familiar with the kinds of files available for downloading and how to protect your computer from virus infection, you're ready to access online resources. Downloading files from Internet sites can be as simple as clicking a hyperlink or dragging and dropping a file onto your desktop.

If you're viewing a Web page that has files ready to be downloaded (such as **www.irs.gov**), you only need to click the download link to initiate the download process. This opens a dialog box in which you can indicate the folder you want the file to be transferred to. A lot of files you'll want to download (including tax forms) will be PDF files, so in the following exercise, you'll download the installation file for Adobe® Acrobat® (program files are discussed in the following section), the utility used for viewing PDF files:

 Some computer manufacturers provide this type of software on your computer already.

① Open Internet Explorer by clicking **start** and then **Internet**.

② If your computer doesn't connect automatically, manually establish your Internet connection by clicking **start**, **Connect To**, and your dial-up connection.

③ Click in the Address text field.

④ If the URL in the Address field isn't highlighted, press **DELETE** or **BACKSPACE** to clear any existing URL from the Address field.

⑤ Type **www.acrobat.com** and press **ENTER**.

⑥ The Adobe Acrobat Web site opens. Position your mouse pointer over the Downloads link to reveal the download menu selection list and click **Free Acrobat Reader**.

The URL you typed may automatically change to something else much more complicated. Don't be alarmed; it's common for companies to use simple URLs and redirect them to more complex URLs where the content is actually stored.

⑦ The Acrobat Reader information Web page opens. Scroll down and click **Get Acrobat Reader**.

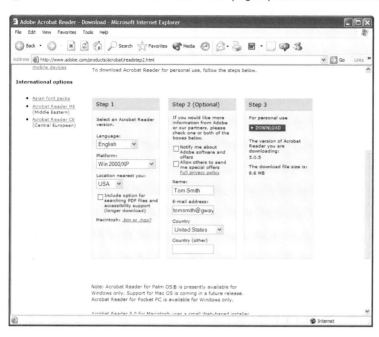

⑧ The Acrobat Reader download Web page opens. Scroll down. In the Step 1 section, use the drop-down lists to select your language, platform (operating system), and the country closest to you. Also, select the **Include option for searching PDF files and accessibility support** check box.

⑨ In the Step 2 section, type your name and e-mail address and select your country from the drop-down list.

 Some Web sites require you to register or at least provide basic information about yourself before you can download files.

⑩ In the Step 3 section, click **Download**.

⑪ After a few moments, the File Download dialog box opens. Click **Save**.

⑫ The Save As dialog box opens. Click the **Desktop** button and then click **Save**.

 When downloading files you can usually accept the file name provided. However, if you want to provide a longer or more descriptive file name, just type it in the file name field before clicking Save.

⑬ The % Completed dialog box shows the progress of the download. Once the download is complete, the dialog box closes automatically.

 If you clear the check box **Close this dialog box when download completes** check box, the dialog box remains open until you close it.

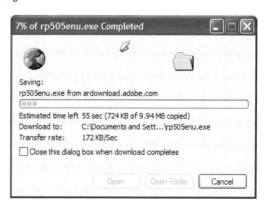

Now the file you downloaded is on your desktop. You can continue surfing the Web or go to your desktop and use, view, or install the downloaded file. You can use this general procedure for downloading any type of file from any Web site.

If you're accessing an FTP site directly through a Web browser, you can use standard file copy procedures to download files. You can drag files to a folder on your hard drive, use the standard Copy and Paste commands, or choose the Copy To Folder command from a file's shortcut menu.

Programs

Downloading programs is a great way to add new tools and capabilities to your computer. However, there are a few things to keep in mind when downloading programs. The most important thing is the use restrictions for the type of software. There are three types of software:

✦ Purchased software, also known as *commercial software*, is any program you have to pay for to use. If you don't pay for it, you can't use it.

 Before you can download purchased software, you'll have to pay for it by supplying a credit card number and billing information.

✦ Shareware is a try-before-you-buy type of software. You're usually granted 30 to 90 days to try out the software before the program stops working. If you fail to purchase a valid use license before the trial period expires, you're no longer able to legally use the program, even if it continues to work.

✦ Freeware is software you can use without paying for it.

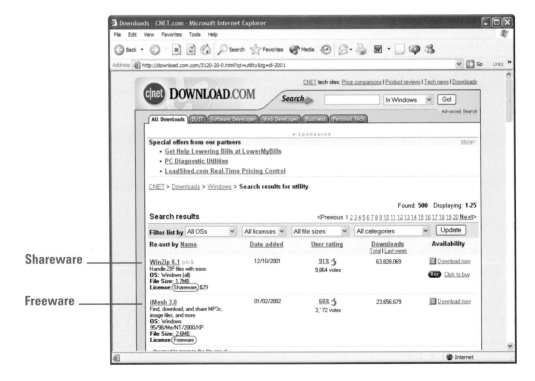

Most software is clearly labeled as to what type it is. In fact, you usually must pay for commercial software before you can download it or even install it. Shareware includes a reminder that you have a limited time to try the product before your test period expires; you usually see it each time you open the program. All software that you install on your computer will be commercial, shareware, or freeware; this includes utilities, games, screen savers, and so on. Be sure you know which type of software you're installing and always comply with any restrictions that apply.

You can locate software all over the Internet. Commercial software can be found through the product's manufacturer or through an online software retail outlet. Shareware and freeware programs are usually found at online software repositories.

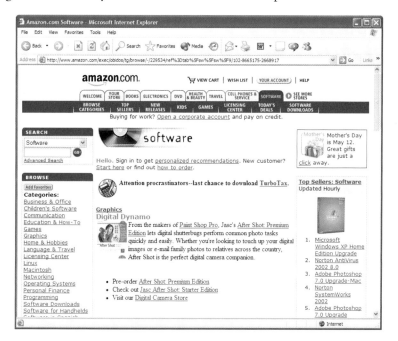

To practice downloading files with Internet Explorer, go to the CD-ROM segment *Internet Explorer: Downloading Files.*

To find out where you can get URLs for online software retail outlet and online software repositories, see the table at the end of this chapter.

Games

Just as there are hundreds of interactive games that you can play online, there are hundreds of games you can download to play on your computer without being connected to the Internet. If you already know the name of a game you want, just use a search engine to find it. If you want to look for a type of game or for games in general, use a search engine with appropriate keywords, such as "card games", "car games", "educational games", or just "games".

To download a game to your computer, usually all you have to do is click a hyperlink for the game. If it's commercial software, you'll have to pay for the software before you can download the program.

 Games are software, so they're commercial, shareware, or freeware. Be sure to comply with any software-specific restrictions.

 To find URLs for places to look for online games, see the table at the end of this chapter.

Research Material and Other Documents

Downloading documents, tax forms, white papers, and so on is usually a matter of clicking a hyperlink and selecting the destination folder. The real key to downloading document files is having the proper reader. Without the proper reader application, a downloaded document is of little use.

There are several common document file types, including DOC, TXT, RTF, and PDF. Windows XP is equipped to read the first three through WordPad, but if you want to read PDF files, you'll need to install the Adobe Acrobat Reader (see "Downloading Step-By-Step" earlier in this chapter).

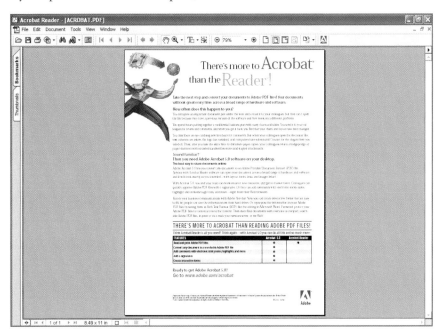

If you discover a document type that you cannot open with your existing reader applications, try searching the Internet using the file extension of the unknown document as the keyword. Often, finding a reader tool is as simple as performing a search for it on the Internet.

In addition to the four common document types, there's another emerging document transmission mechanism known as electronic books, or eBooks. EBooks consist of the text of a book in a special file that is formatted so it looks like a printed book, but on a computer or hand-held computer screen. Many companies, online bookstores, and book publishers are distributing books electronically. In most cases, you must purchase the eBook before downloading it, but there are some freeware or first-chapters-free eBooks available. There are several formats for electronic books and you must have the correct reader or viewer to view the contents.

Microsoft has an eBook viewer called the Microsoft Reader. You can obtain eBooks for the Microsoft Reader through a number of online sites.

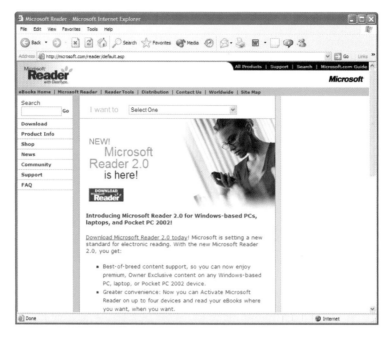

If the documentation you need is not in a downloadable file format but rather is displayed as the text of a Web page, there are still ways to download it to your computer. First, you can choose the **Save As** command from the File menu in Internet Explorer to make a copy of the HTML file currently being viewed. However, you'll save only the text; the images won't be included. Another method is to select the text within Internet Explorer and cut and paste it into a WordPad document. This option also saves only the text, not the images. If you need the images as well, you must either save each image individually (see next section) or make the entire page available offline.

Making a Web page available offline is simple. Click the **Add to Favorites** command while viewing the Web page and then select the **Make Available Offline** check box before clicking OK in the Add Favorite dialog box. This action instructs Internet Explorer to copy the Web page and all of the page's non-text elements, such as graphics, to your computer's hard drive. The next time you attempt to access the Web page using the Favorites menu, you'll be viewing the Web page from the stored version on your hard drive.

Pictures

Downloading pictures is typically accomplished using one of two methods. If the picture is on a Web site or FTP site as a link, click the link to initiate the download just as with any other type of file.

If the picture is displayed as an element on a Web page, you can grab it and save it to your computer. To grab an image from a Web page, right-click over the image and choose one of the following commands:

✦ **Save Picture As.** This command is used to save the image file to your computer. You're prompted for a file name and the folder location to save the image file.

✦ **E-mail Picture.** This command is used to e-mail the image file. To use this command, an e-mail program must be configured on your computer. (See Chapter 8.)

✦ **Print Picture.** This command prints the image. Your printer must be configured to use this command.

✦ **Set as Background.** This command saves the image file to your computer as Internet Explorer Wallpaper.bmp and then the image is set as the desktop wallpaper or background image. If you select this command for another image, the existing wallpaper or background is replaced.

✦ **Set as Desktop Item.** This command sets the image as an Active Desktop element on your desktop. The image remains as a link to its original location. Avoid using this command because you don't want links to somewhere else on your desktop.

 To find a picture of a particular image, you can use a search engine. Start by using keywords that describe the content or subject of the picture, such as "sailboat", "yellow tulips", or "boy with dog". If you don't find what you want, look for picture catalogs or image clearinghouses by searching for "pictures", "images", or "graphics".

Once an image is on your computer, you'll need the right program to view it. If it's a common image format such as BMP, GIF, JPG, or TIF, you can view it through your Web browser. If it's some other image file type, you may need to use a search engine to look for a specialized viewer.

In this exercise, you'll download and save an image using Internet Explorer:

❶ To open Internet Explorer click **start** and then **Internet**. If your computer doesn't connect automatically, manually establish your Internet connection by clicking **start**, **Connect To**, and your dial-up connection.

❷ Click in the Address text field.

❸ If the URL in the Address field isn't highlighted, press **DELETE** or **BACKSPACE** to clear any existing URL from the Address field.

④ Type **www.gateway.com/learningdownloads** and press **ENTER**.

⑤ Scroll to the Digital Images that you can Download section.

⑥ Right-click on the image you want to download and choose **Save Picture As**.

⑦ The Save Picture dialog box opens. Choose where you want to save the picture and rename the picture if you'd like. (Windows XP defaults to the My Pictures folder.)

⑧ Click **Save**. The picture is saved to your computer.

 This process is similar for all browsers although the menu options you choose may be slightly different.

Other Downloads

Downloading anything from the Internet is simple, whether it's a program, a picture, a screen saver, a movie, an animation file, or even an audio file. You only need to make sure you have a viewer or player for the file. If you don't have a viewer/player for a file, just search for the file type with a search engine to locate one.

 When downloading files in multiuser operating systems such as Windows XP, you must be aware that multiple users have their own accounts on the same computer. Items saved to your My Documents, My Pictures, or My Music folder are not accessible to other users. If you wish to have downloaded files available to other users, you can save them in the Shared Documents folder.

Go to the CD-ROM and select the segment:

✦ *Anti-Virus Software* to know more about how to avoid getting viruses from downloaded Internet files.

✦ *Security: Risks and Solutions* to learn more about security and system protection.

✦ *Internet Explorer: Downloading Files* to practice downloading files with Internet Explorer.

Go online to **www.LearnwithGateway.com** and log on to select:

✦ *Internet Links and Resources*

   ✦ *Archive tools*

   ✦ *File Extensions*

   ✦ *Software Retailers and Repositories*

   ✦ *Online Games*

✦ *FAQs*

With the *Survive & Thrive* series, refer to *Create and Share Digital Photos* for more information on:

✦ *Downloading photos*

Refer to *Use Your PC to Explore Digital Music* for more information on:

✦ *Downloading music*

Gateway offers a hands-on training course that covers many of the topics in this chapter. Additional fees may apply. Call **888-852-4821** for enrollment information. If applicable, please have your customer ID and order number ready when you call.

6

Exploring AOL and the Internet

J ust as you can probably find your way to an address in an unfamiliar part of town without using a map or directions, you can probably find what you want online without any navigational tools or guidance. In both cases, though, using the right resources will get you to your destination more efficiently and with less hassle. The America Online service, or AOL as it's often called, is a popular Internet online service that provides its members with thousands of resources to quickly find the information they want online.

This chapter shows you how to connect to the Internet using the America Online service and, once you're connected, how to find the information you desire. Whether you want to find a hot new Web site, tomorrow's weather forecast, or the population of Bangladesh, the America Online service makes finding what you want online a breeze.

Connecting to the America Online Service

Once your America Online account is set up, you can get started. Upon installation, America Online conveniently sets up shortcuts on your computer for quick access. By default, a shortcut to the America Online service is located at the top of the All Programs menu, and within the America Online submenu. When you sign on to America Online for the first time, you'll be given the option to make America Online your preferred application, or default, for browsing the Web and using e-mail. If you set up AOL as your default Internet service, shortcuts to AOL and AOL e-mail will be conveniently placed at the top of your start menu. To get started with the America Online service, do the following:

1 Click the **start** button, point to **All Programs**, and select **America Online**.

② The America Online software opens and prompts you to connect. Your ScreenName may appear in the Select ScreenName box.

If you've connected to America Online before and have already created additional screen names, you may need to click the drop-down arrow to select the screen name you want to use for this online session. Click the Select ScreenName drop-down arrow to view the available screen names, if necessary. Click to select your screen name.

③ If you're prompted for a password, click inside the Type Password text box and type the password you created for the screen name. For security reasons, the password will appear as *****.

④ Click the SIGN ON button to establish a connection with America Online.

7

⑤ Watch the status bar to monitor the connection process.

Your modem will initialize, dial, and connect to your local access number. If the access number is busy, a message will appear in a white box in the upper-left corner of the screen displaying dialing status. The software will automatically try to connect again.

To practice connecting to the America Online service, go to the Web segment *AOL Connecting* in the AOL course.

More About . . . Saving Your Password

If a Password Store Information box appears, you can choose to have the America Online service remember your password so you don't have to enter it every time you connect. To save your password, type the password in the box, reenter it to confirm it, and then click OK. A message box is displayed to confirm that your password has been saved for sign on. Click OK to close the message box. If you're sharing your computer with others or with children, you may not want to store your password. If you don't want to save your password, simply click Cancel.

Using the America Online Service to Navigate the Web

Once you're connected to the America Online service, you'll want to familiarize yourself with the interface, or user environment, as well as the Welcome screen, which is the opening page that serves as a directory or table of contents to other exciting and convenient links.

Becoming Familiar with the America Online Toolbars and Menu Bars

The America Online service provides an AOL toolbar, menu bar, and navigation bar to make viewing and navigating the Web easier.

 To tour the key features of the America Online service, go to the Web segment *AOL Introduction* in the AOL course.

Table 7-1 lists each of the sections of the AOL toolbar and its function.

Table 7-1 Sections of the AOL toolbar and their functions.

Section	Function
Mail	Enables you to access more than 13 features related to e-mail, including the most popular, Read mail and Write mail.
People	Includes features such as Instant Message and Chat, which enable you to meet people and stay in touch with friends, relatives, and AOL members.
Services	Enables you to access many of AOL's useful online tools, such as Shop@AOL, My Calendar, Maps & Directions, and Travel Reservations.
Settings	Provides features that enable you to customize the AOL software to meet your needs, such as Parental Controls and Screen Names.
Favorites	Gathers shortcuts to your favorite places on the AOL® service and the Web.

Browsing America Online and the Web will be easier if you become familiar with some of the basic toolbar buttons. You can do so by following these steps:

① View the America Online menu bar, AOL toolbar, and navigation bar.

Menu bar   AOL toolbar   AOL Channels

Address bar (where the user enters the text)

Welcome screen

② You can use the AOL toolbar to access the most popular features of the America Online service. Notice that the AOL toolbar contains color-coded sections. Each section is categorized and includes a drop-down menu and one or more buttons that you can use to access the most popular features.

③ Move the mouse pointer slowly across each of the drop-down menus and buttons on the AOL toolbar to view the function of each.

④ The navigation bar provides you with features to assist you in moving around the AOL service and the Web. Identify the following control buttons on the navigation bar:

✦ **Channels**. If the AOL Channels windows is not viewable, click the Channels button to show it. You can useChannels, which are discussed in detail later in this chapter, to search for content on America Online.

✦ Move the mouse pointer over the AOL Keyword button. Click the AOL Keyword button to open the Keywords window, which enables you to type an America Online Keyword and go to the associated area online. AOL Keywords will be covered later in this chapter.

✦ **Back/Forward**. The Back button moves you back through the pages you've viewed in the current session, one page at a time. Use this if you remember seeing something you want to see again but are not sure on which page it appeared. After you've backtracked to recently viewed pages, the Forward button is available to move you forward through sequentially accessed pages.

✦ **Stop.** Click the Stop button to stop a Web page from loading in the browser window. Because some pages with heavy graphics take longer to load, you may sometimes want to stop loading the page and read or click links on the partially loaded page.

✦ **Refresh.** Click the Refresh button to reload the entire page when a Web page does not completely load in the browser window.

⑤ View the Address bar. The Address bar is the text box used to enter or identify a Web page's address. To use the Address bar, you click inside the Address bar, type a Web address, and click the Go button or press ENTER to go to the desired AOL area or Web page. To return to any of the last 25 AOL areas or Web pages you've visited, click the drop-down arrow to the right of the Address bar and select the appropriate item.

⑥ Move the mouse pointer over the Search button. The Search button is used to execute a search by subject category. To perform a search, click inside the Search text box, type a word or phrase on which you want to search, and click the Search button.

 To see the America Online toolbar and navigation features, go to the CD-ROM segment *AOL: Navigating the Web.*

 To see the America Online toolbar and navigation features, go to the Web segment *AOL: Navigating the Web.*

Quick Access with the AOL Companion

When you are connected to the America Online service, a small window appears by default. This window is called the AOL Companion.

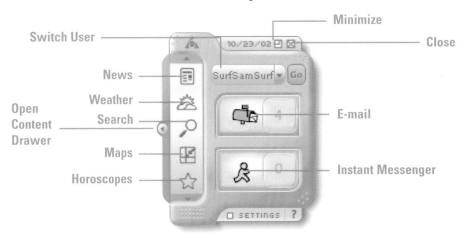

You can use the AOL Companion as a quick way to access the America Online Service from your desktop. You can easily get to your favorite AOL features, including the Buddy List® window, News headlines, your local weather and many other America Online applications. The AOL Companion also helps you stay on top your AOL e-mail and Instant Messages.

The following steps show you how to use the AOL Companion:

① If the America Online service is currently running, click the Close button (the "X" in the upper right corner) to log off and exit.

② Click on the Open Content Drawer button on the left side of the AOL Companion. The Content Drawer opens.

 Move your mouse over the Weather button. When the Weather button starts to animate, click it. The Content Drawer displays the weather according to your zip code settings.

 Click on the Open Content Drawer button again, closing the Content Drawer.

⑤ Click the Change Zip Code link the AOL Companion. The America Online service will launch.

⑥ Sign on to the America Online service. Once you have signed on, you are automatically taken to the Change Your City by Zip Code window. Click the "X" in the top right of the window to close it.

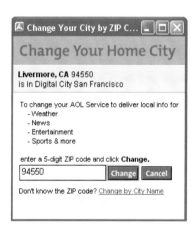

When you sign on to the America Online service, you will notice that the AOL Companion changes size. The AOL Companion automatically minimizes when you start the America Online service. To maximize the AOL Companion, click the Maximize button located in the upper right of the AOL Companion.

To learn more about using AOL Companion, go to the Web segment *AOL: Companion.*

7

Surfing the America Online Service for the First Time

When the America Online service connects and the Welcome screen appears, several small windows will open on top of the Welcome screen to provide quick access to America Online service features such as your Buddy List®, Channels, news events, and special offers. To use the America Online service for the first time, follow these steps:

① View the Welcome to AOL 8.0 screen. This window opens the first time you connect to America Online.

② Click the Close button (the button with X in the upper-right corner) of the AOL 8.0 Welcome screen. The Welcome screen minimizes to the bottom left. Re-open the Welcome screen by clicking the Restore Up button (the button with the two small windows in the upper-right corner) or by double-clicking the Title Bar.

③ Click the title bar of the Buddy List window to activate it. You can use this window to communicate online with your family and friends by using the Instant Messenger feature or chat.

④ Click the Close button in the upper-right corner of the Buddy List window.

⑤ Click the title bar of the AOL Channels menu to activate it. AOL uses Channels to organize its content into categories of information. You can use the AOL Channels menu to quickly navigate to any AOL Channel.

 If your computer's speakers are turned on, you might sometimes receive a message, accompanied by an audio sound, asking, "Do you wish to continue to stay online?" Click Yes to stay connected.

⑥ Look at the Welcome screen and note the strategic headings and hyperlinks.

⑦ In addition to traditional modem connections, AOL provides a high-speed internet connection service. AOL Broadband uses high-speed DSL, cable, or satellite connections to provide many enhanced features. If you already have a high-speed connection, you will see enhanced broadband features and links on your Welcome screen. Clicking on links in this area will take you directly to video and audio content featured by AOL Broadband. If you have a high-speed connection, view the Better on AOL Broadband feature.

⑧ Look at the large icons along the left side of the Welcome screen. The icons and their features are as follows:

✦ You've Got Mail/Mail Center. As soon as you see the Welcome screen, you'll know whether you have e-mail. If you do, you'll hear "You've Got Mail" when you sign-on and the icon will read "You've Got Mail" and contain a raised red flag. Simply click the icon to access your Online Mailbox. If you don't have mail, the icon will read "Mail Center." Click the icon to access the Mail Center.

✦ You've Got Pictures™ service. This feature enables you to get your pictures delivered right to your America Online service account, and is particularly useful if you use a digital camera. You can easily upload, store, and share your photos for free. When you go to get your film developed, you must ask for the You've Got Pictures service. Look for the associated check box on the film-processing envelope. You must also fill in your e-mail address on the envelope. After a few days, when you log in to the America Online service, you'll hear "You've Got Pictures" when you sign-on, and the Welcome screen will display the You've Got Pictures icon with a film canister icon showing exposed film. This indicates that your pictures are available for viewing. To view the pictures, simply click the You've Got Pictures icon.

✦ People & Chat. When you click the People & Chat icon, the People Connection window opens. You can use People Connection for person-to-person interaction.

9. Move the mouse pointer across the page. Note the physical change of the pointer as it moves across a hyperlink. The pointing arrow changes to a hand. When the pointer moves off the hyperlink, it returns to the arrow shape.

10. On the bottom left side of the Welcome screen, click Change This Screen. The Change My Welcome screen window opens.

11. Move the mouse pointer over Welcome screen 1 and click it. A new window opens, giving you a preview of the new Welcome screen. Click the green Select This Screen button. Another window opens asking you to confirm your selection. Click OK, and your Welcome screen will change to Welcome screen 1.

7

No matter which Welcome screen style you select, you will continue to see links for e-mail, top news, local news and weather.

12. On the bottom left, under At a Glance, click the Sports Scores button. The AOL Sports Scoreboards page opens.

13. Click on the AOL Sports logo in the top left of the window. The AOL Sports Main page opens.

14. On the navigation bar, click the Back button to return to the AOL Sports Scoreboards page.

15. Click the Close button to return to the America Online Welcome screen.

Using America Online Channels

AOL 8.0 offers 20 different information Channels, which bring together original content and programming from the America Online service, information from leading media partners, and links to related areas on the Web. With AOL 8.0, these Channels are even easier for you to reach, whenever you want, from a "menu" located on the redesigned navigation toolbar. With just a glance, you can quickly connect to shopping resources and stores; access news and information on personal finance, careers, health, and parenting; get the latest music and games, and more—from wherever you are online. The following are the AOL Channels available with AOL 8.0, and what they offer:

✦ **Autos.** The AOL Auto Channel has all the features and functionality you need to ease the burden of the traditional car-buying process, from enhanced research tools to price quotes from local dealers. You'll also find easy-to-use calculators and decision guides to help you determine how much you can afford to pay for a car, what your monthly payments will be, trade-in values, information on financing, and much more.

✦ **Careers & Work.** The AOL Careers & Work Channel makes it easier for professionals to find jobs or advance their careers by inspiring, educating, and equipping them with the tools they need to be more productive and successful. This Channel enables you to create new businesses and professional opportunities or expand existing ventures.

✦ **Computer Center.** Whether for downloading software or getting the low-down on hardware and technology, the AOL Computer Center is a comprehensive resource for novice, intermediate, or advanced computer users.

✦ **Entertainment.** The AOL Entertainment Channel delivers the most useful information about movies, TV, and celebrities by combining AOL's exclusive content with the Web's best offerings. Exclusive features, interactive content, live events, and fan forums are only a few of the ways that the Entertainment Channel enriches your entertainment experience. If you want to read about the latest happenings in the world of entertainment, click the Entertainment Channel.

◆ **Games.** The AOL Games Channel delivers what online game players want most: ease of use, fun, and friends. AOL Games is the most popular mainstream audience gaming site and the largest game destination in cyberspace.

◆ **Health.** The AOL Health Channel provides you with a vast selection of resources covering a wide range of health issues, from maintaining a healthy lifestyle to coping with an illness. Medical references and assistance from support groups and experts are available 24 hours a day.

◆ **House & Home.** The AOL House & Home Channel is a one-stop resource for "everything home" on the Web.

◆ **International.** The AOL International Channel brings cultural communities together, delivers news and information about hundreds of countries, and forms a bridge to AOL's other services around the world.

◆ **Kids Only.** From clubs to games to homework help, the AOL Kids Only Channel is really a service unto itself. Children with Kids Only accounts get a personalized Welcome screen and can explore the Channels made just for them.

7

◆ **Local Guide.** The #1 online local content provider and guide, Digital City® provides AOL members and Internet users with locally relevant news, community resources, entertainment, and commerce in an engaging, easy-to-use format. Digital City now covers more than 200 metropolitan areas in the U.S. and partners with some of the nation's top local media companies to deliver branded local news, weather, sports, traffic, and entertainment. To access the Local Guide Channel, you can also use the **AOL Keyword: Digital City.**

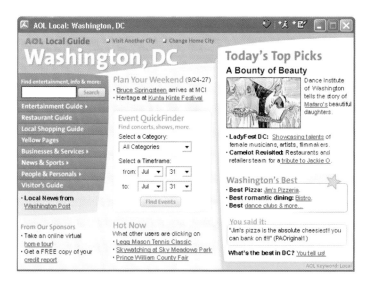

✦ **Music.** The AOL Music Channel is a popular destination for fans of all kinds of music, from country to hip-hop to Latin and everything in between. The AOL Music Channel gives you access to the music and artists you love with news and reviews, photos, tour information, artist bios, and digital music downloads.

✦ **News.** The AOL News Channel is the #1 online source for news in cyberspace, visited by millions of members every day. With updates around the clock from the world's most trusted news sources, the AOL News Channel provides headlines and in-depth coverage in a convenient, easy-to-use format.

✦ **Parenting.** The AOL Parenting Channel provides information, tools, and advice about how to enrich and enjoy our precious family relationships. Experts and members alike share thoughts and experiences that others use in their daily lives.

✦ **Personal Finance.** The AOL Personal Finance Channel equips you with the best selection of online financial resources, tools, services, and community features. Visitors use the area to make informed decisions and safely conduct transactions. To access the Personal Finance Channel, you can also use the **AOL Keyword: PF.**

✦ **Research & Learn.** Offering everything from homework help to online courses, the AOL Research & Learn Channel provides students and lifelong learners with a one-stop shop for doing research and learning more about your topics of interest.

- **Shopping.** The AOL Shopping Channel takes the convenience of catalog shopping to the interactive medium, making browsing and purchasing safe and easy. AOL certified merchants' 100% satisfaction guarantee ensures total satisfaction for shoppers. In addition, the Shopping Channel includes a number of valuable features:

  Quick Checkout. Saves you time while shopping online by securely storing billing and shipping information. When it's time to check out at a participating AOL merchant, you don't have to enter your billing and shipping information. Quick Checkout takes care of that for you. You can sign up for this service at **AOL Keyword: Quick Checkout.**

  Reminder Service. You can sign up for the free Reminder Service, which allows you to save important dates, such as birthdays and anniversaries, and then sends you a reminder before the date so you don't miss it. When you receive that reminder, you'll have plenty of time to use The AOL Shopping Channel for all those special people. To access the Reminder Service, you can use **AOL Keyword: Reminder.**

  AOL Shopping Guarantee. When you purchase an item, do you ever worry about what type of guarantee is included? Well, worry no more. The America Online service provides you with a 100% satisfaction guarantee. By requiring that each of its certified merchants meets its high standards for customer service, security, and privacy protection, you can be sure that the America Online Service guarantees your satisfaction on any purchase you make online. See **AOL Keyword: Guarantee.**

You might be wondering how safe it is to shop online with Shop@AOL. Well, fear not, because AOL has taken numerous measures and made it a top priority to ensure that your credit card information is kept safe and secure.

- **Sports.** The AOL Sports Channel is the world's most popular Internet/online sports site, having attracted a loyal following of fans seeking the latest sports news, scores, and statistics. The Sports channel provides visitors with a place to interact with other fans, fantasy players, and sports newsmakers.

- **Teens.** The AOL Teens Channel encompasses all that is compelling to young teens, both online and offline, and reflects the qualities of its target audience: in touch, intelligent, involved, and fun.

♦ **Travel.** Emphasizing convenience, content, and community, the AOL Travel Channel offers you a comprehensive travel service, with everything from secure online reservations to great trip-planning tools, resources, and advice.

♦ **Women.** The AOL Womens' Channel is the online home of a friendly, supportive community housing information to enrich the lives of women.

To use America Online Channels, follow these steps:

1. Look at the AOL Channels menu, noting the categorized links. You can use this menu to search for content on the America Online service.

2. Move the mouse pointer over a channel, for example, the Welcome Channel. Now move the mouse over the small arrow to the right of the channel. Click the arrow. A menu appears, indicating the contents of that Channel. Feel free to explore other areas.

Getting Help

The America Online service provides you with many ways to get help when you're online, including AOL Help and AOL Anywhere Help. To access AOL Help, click Help and select AOL Help. AOL Help is a non-Web help system that you can use to find the answers to your most frequently asked questions about AOL.

 To explore the features of the Help function within the America Online service, go to the Web segment *AOL Help* in the AOL course.

Another form of help you can use is AOL Anywhere Help, which provides you with general information to assist you in getting up and running when you first start using the America Online service.

During the following exercise, you'll access AOL Help and the AOL Anywhere Help Web page:

1. Click AOL Help on the menu bar, or press F1 to open the AOL Help page.

 You can also use AOL Keyword: Help.

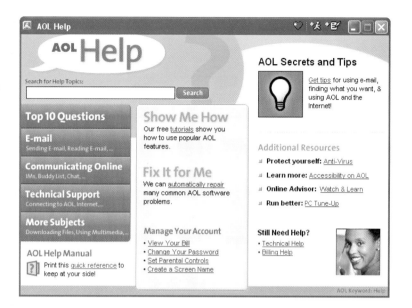

2 The left side of the page displays five Help buttons to get you started. Click the More Subjects button.

3 The More Subjects window opens. This window has several general categories for you to choose from. From here, all you have to do is click a subject on the left and click one of the associated articles on the right.

4 Click the Close button of the More Things page to return to the AOL Help screen. Note that there are many other help topics listed here. Click the Close button to close Help and return to the Welcome screen.

5 For assistance, you can also use AOL Anywhere Help, which is accessible from outside your AOL account. Click inside the Address bar and type www.aol.com/nethelp/home.html.

6 Click Go. The AOL Anywhere Help page loads into the browser window.

7 From here, you can access help on various topics.

8 Under AOL Anywhere Help, click the Top 20 AOL Member Questions hyperlink.

Marking a Favorite Place

As you surf online, you may find certain sites that you know you'll want to visit frequently. You can mark Web pages for later reference just as you can mark pages in a book or magazine you're reading. The Favorites button on the AOL toolbar provides several menu functions that allow you to add the current site to a quickly accessible list.

1 Open the Web page you want to add as a favorite site.

2 Click the red heart on the title bar to identify this Web page as a favorite site. The America Online window opens.

Favorite Place
(red heart)

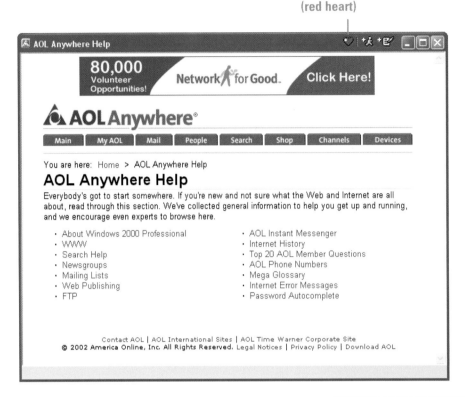

3 Click Add to Favorites, then click Favorite Places on the menu that appears.

If your speakers are turned on, you'll hear a sound indicating that the Web page has been added to Favorites.

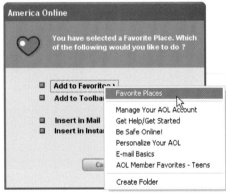

4 Click the Favorites button on the AOL toolbar. The Web page appears as the last entry on the menu.

5 Click the Favorites button again to close the menu.

To be able to add favorite places to your America Online service, go to the CD-ROM segment *AOL Favorites: Adding Web Pages*.

Editing Favorite Entries

When you're saving a site to Favorites, sometimes the default site name reference is confusing or just too long. America Online allows you to edit the name of favorite entries to make them more meaningful to you:

① Click the Favorites button on the AOL toolbar.

② Choose Favorite Places from the menu.

 Links to favorite Web pages can also be added to e-mail messages.

③ A Favorite Places window opens. In that window, select the Favorite Place you want to rename.

④ Click the Edit button and a third window opens.

⑤ In the Enter the Place's Description text box, select the existing text and type a new name for that Favorite Place.

⑥ Click OK. Verify that the entry in the Favorite Places window reflects your edit.

 To delete the Favorite Place you just created, click the item in the Favorite Places window and then click the Delete button.

7 The Favorite Place button can also be used to add links to Instant Messages and e-mail or to add a link to a favorite Web page as an icon on the toolbar. Open the Web page you want to add as a link.

8 Click the Favorite Place button. The America Online window opens.

 If your screen resolution is set lower than 1024 by 768 pixels, a message appears stating that adding an item will make the toolbar too large for the screen. An icon will have to be deleted from the toolbar before you can add an icon.

9 Click Add to Toolbar.

10 The Select Icon window dialog box opens. Click an icon and type a name for the Web page in the Label (required) text box.

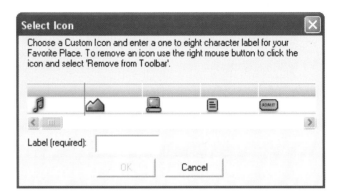

11 Click OK from the menu. You'll see the icon on your toolbar.

 An icon can be deleted from the toolbar by right-clicking it and selecting the Remove from Toolbar option.

12 Click the Close button in the upper-right corner of the Web page window to return to the Welcome screen.

Searching for Information Using the America Online Service

The America Online service provides several convenient search tools to help you locate information on the Web. The America Online service provides a handy, comprehensive, and easy-to-use search engine that allows you to use an AOL Keyword or phrase to move around quickly online, eliminating the need to enter a long Web address. AOL Keywords appear in the lower-right corner of a window. To quickly search for and retrieve a specific stock's current performance information, you can use the Quotes button on the America

Online Welcome screen. AOL allows you to search within the community using subject categories. The search techniques described in the previous chapters can also be used.

 To practice using the search features of AOL, go to the Web segment *AOL Keywords* in the AOL course.

Using a Keyword

To execute a search, you can enter a key word or phrase in the AOL Keyword text box, and the search engine is given the command to find the word or phrase in the Web pages contained in its databases. When the search is complete, an America Online page that contains the matching Keyword opens.

There are a few things you can do if you're unsure of a Keyword. First, in the Keyword window, click Keyword List to access Keywords, including the 10 most popular ones. You can also just try entering a word that you think might be a Keyword. You'll be surprised at how often you get the results you're looking for. Let's work with an example:

1 In the Address bar, type weather and press ENTER. The AOL News: National Weather page opens.

2 Look at the lower-right corner of the window. Notice the text AOL Keyword: Weather.

 The AOL Weather preferences may have been set previously to display the local weather instead of national weather. If this is the case, the AOL Keyword: Weather may not appear in lower-right corner of the window.

3 On the navigation bar, click AOL Keyword to open the AOL Keywords window.

4 Click the Keyword List hyperlink to open a new, expanded version of the AOL Keywords window.

5 You can use this window to access a list of the most popular Keywords, an alphabetical list of Keywords, or a list of Keywords by Channel and to perform other types of Keyword searches.

6 Click the Close button in all open windows to return to the Welcome screen.

Searching by Subject Category

To execute a search by subject category, follow these steps:

1 Click the Search button to the right of the Address bar. The AOL Search: Home page opens.

2 Click the Autos hyperlink. A list of subcategories appears for a variety of auto topics.

Buyers Guides link

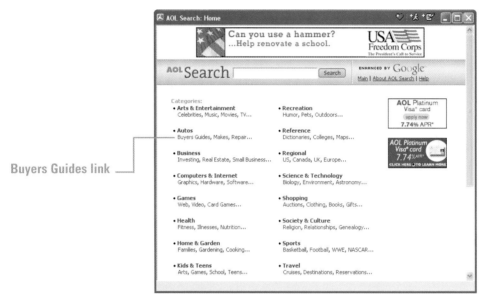

 There are also independent search engines that may offer different search criteria, categories, and subject directories.

3 Click the Buyers Guides hyperlink. A list of subcategories appears listing buyers guides options.

New (in Subcategories)

4 Click the New hyperlink to view the different makes of new vehicles.

5 Click the Close button in the upper-right corner of the New window to return to the Welcome screen.

Go to the CD-ROM and select the segment:

✦ *AOL: Navigating the Web*

✦ *AOL Favorites: Adding Web Pages*

✦ *AOL: Downloading Files*

Go online to www.LearnwithGateway.com and log on to select:

✦ *America Online course*

✦ *Internet Links and Resources*

✦ *FAQs*

Gateway offers a hands-on training course that covers many of the topics in this chapter. Additional fees may apply. Call 888-852-4821 for enrollment information. If applicable, please have your customer ID and order number ready when you call.

Communicating with Friends and Family

W hereas most Web and FTP sites are designed to be accessed by many people—even millions—e-mail and other forms of Internet communication serve individuals. The difference between viewing an Internet site and reading an e-mail message is similar to the difference between looking at a glossy bulk-rate catalog in the mail and receiving a crisp first-class letter from your best friend. Some Web sites are useful and fun, but unlike that letter that you can't wait to open and read several times, they aren't addressed directly to you and you alone.

Of course, unlike that first-class letter that took four days to reach your mailbox, most Internet communication is often almost instantaneous. It allows you to stay in closer contact with family, friends, and business associates, and lets you make new acquaintances—without leaving your home.

Introducing Online Communications

Once you turn on your computer and connect to the Internet, there are several ways you can express yourself online. The four most direct and personal ways are e-mail, instant messaging, chat, and newsgroups.

✦ **E-mail.** An *e-mail (electronic mail)* message is written communication (similar to a letter) that is sent from one computer to another. E-mail is usually just text, but it can include pictures, formatting, and animation. You can also attach any type of file, such as programs, music files, or digital photographs, to an e-mail message. E-mail is covered later in this chapter.

✦ **Instant Messaging.** *Instant messaging programs* enable people to send short messages to online recipients in real time. By using the contact list that identifies the screen names of your friends, family, and associates, you can identify when one of them is online and exchange messages that travel instantaneously. The MSN Messenger tool is covered in Chapter 10. AOL Instant Messenger is covered in Chapter 11.

- ✦ **Chat.** A *chat room* is a virtual space within the Internet where two or more users chat (converse) in real time. In chat rooms, you can meet others from around the world who share the same interests as you. Chat rooms are often created to support specific interests, such as pets, hobbies, health concerns, and so on. Users chat by entering a chat room and typing messages that appear on the screens of all those chatting together. The MSN Messenger Chat is covered in Chapter 10. AOL chat rooms are covered in Chapter 11.

- ✦ **Newsgroups.** *Newsgroups* are Usenet discussion groups whose members post articles and messages that pertain to specific topics of interest. (Usenet is the name of the system that contains newsgroups.) Functioning like a bulletin board in a public building, newsgroups let you choose which topics you want to read. You can participate by posting messages and responding to messages posted by others.

 To find out where you can read more about Usenet Newsgroups, see the table at the end of this chapter.

Communicating via E-mail

Although e-mail can't replace real-time communication (telephone, video conferencing, or the sound of another person's voice), it does open up many new avenues for interaction. Using e-mail, you can exchange messages with people next door or across the globe.

To send and receive e-mail, you need to have an *e-mail client program* on your computer. There are many to choose from. Every Windows operating system since Windows 95 has included a version of Outlook Express. Some alternative e-mail clients are Qualcomm's Eudora, Microsoft Outlook (included with Microsoft Office), and the America Online service. (AOL e-mail is covered in Chapter 9.)

 Microsoft Outlook is similar to Outlook Express but contains additional features.

Although many e-mail clients include unique features or extended capabilities designed to entice users, every e-mail client shares a set of common functions. We assume you already have Outlook Express on your computer, so we'll use it as our primary example and teaching tool for this chapter. After you learn how to use Outlook Express, you can apply that knowledge to any other e-mail client you might encounter.

In addition to the e-mail client, you also need an *e-mail account* with an *e-mail address.* An e-mail account is a service you get from an ISP (Internet service provider) or online service. An e-mail address is a unique address other people use to send you messages. An e-mail address always includes a user name and a special ISP or company domain name separated by the @ sign. For example, bobsmith@gway.com is an e-mail address. When you sign up with an ISP or online service, your account includes at least one e-mail address.

 Often your ISP or online service allows you to have more than one e-mail address so every person in your household can have a unique address.

Exploring the Structure of an E-mail Message

A simple e-mail message consists of the message header and the message body. In the header, the author enters a brief description of the contents or purpose of the message and the e-mail addresses of all recipients. The message body contains the actual message.

Figure 8-1 provides a sample welcome e-mail message from the Microsoft Outlook Express Team. Once the message is read, the recipient can choose to delete it, forward it to someone else, reply to the sender, or simply close the message to keep it. The Reply All option sends the reply message to all message recipients if there's more than one e-mail address in the header portion of the message.

Figure 8-1 An e-mail message.

Configuring Your E-mail Client

One of the most important services an ISP or online service provides is an e-mail account. When you have an e-mail account, you can use your ISP or online service's *mail servers* to send and receive e-mail. Mail servers are computers that manage all the incoming and outgoing mail. Before you can do so, however, you must configure your e-mail client to communicate with these mail servers. To do this, you'll need a few pieces of information from your ISP or online service (contact customer service for assistance, if necessary):

 Don't worry if some of the following items sound strange and unfamiliar; they're common e-mail services used to store your e-mail for you so you can read it on your computer. Your ISP or online service will know what they are.

✦ Your exact e-mail address

✦ The user name and password required to access your e-mail

✦ The type of incoming e-mail service used (POP3, IMAP, or HTTP)

✦ The IP address or domain name for your POP3/IMAP/HTTP mail server (This is your incoming mail server.)

 An IP address is a number, such as 192.168.0.1. A domain name, on the other hand, is similar to a URL for Web pages, such as mail.gway.com.

8

✦ The IP address or domain name for your SMTP mail server (This is your outgoing mail server.)

 It's possible that both incoming and outgoing e-mail servers will have the same domain name or IP address, but most ISPs and online services use a separate e-mail server name for each function.

 To set up an e-mail account in Outlook Express, go to the Web segment *E-mail: Setting Up Accounts* in the Internet Explorer course.

Reading a Message

When you receive an e-mail message, Outlook Express lists information about it—such as the sender, the message subject, and the date and time it was received—in the window's upper-right pane, called the *message list*. However, when you open Outlook Express for the first time after configuring it, notice how information—such as the number of unread messages you have waiting, a link to create a new message, access to your address book, and more—appears in the window's workspace. When you use Outlook Express regularly, however, you may not use this screen at all. Instead, you'll probably work from your Inbox. The *Inbox* is where all new messages sent to your e-mail address appear when they are downloaded to your computer.

To view your Inbox, click the **Inbox** icon in the Folders *pane* on the left side of the screen. (A pane is a subsection of a program window or a subsection of the workspace within a program window.) Notice how the workspace changes, as shown in Figure 8-2.

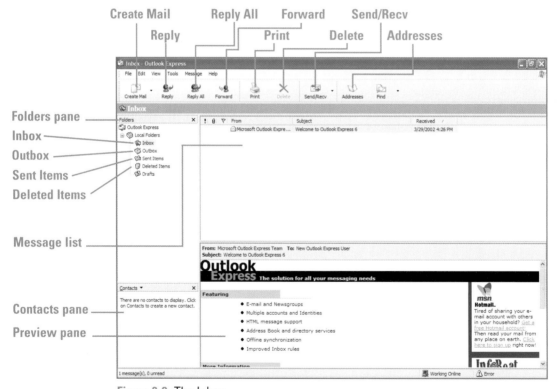

Figure 8-2 The Inbox.

To get the hang of reading messages using Outlook Express, let's look at the default message Microsoft sends to your Inbox the first time you use the program—the one with the subject "Welcome to Outlook Express." Click this message once in the message list;

the message's contents appear in the window's bottom pane. You can use this pane, called the *preview pane*, to quickly preview messages, using the scroll bar on the right side of the pane to view the entire message if you wish. Alternatively, for a better view, you can open the message in a separate window. To do so, follow these steps:

1. Double-click the message in the message list.
2. A new window opens, displaying the contents of the message. Click the Maximize button if the message window is not already maximized.

 Although maximizing the message window helps you read its contents more easily; you may still need to use the scroll bars to see the entire contents of the message.

As shown in the message window in Figure 8-3, four key details about the message appear in the message header:

✦ From. This line reveals the sender's identity.

✦ Date. The date listed here reflects the date and time the sender sent the message to an outgoing e-mail server. This information may differ from what's shown in the main Outlook Express window's message list; the difference in time indicates how long it took the message to travel from the sender to your Inbox.

✦ To. This line denotes the identity of the recipient.

✦ Subject. The Subject line provides a way for the sender to identify, categorize, or label an outgoing e-mail message.

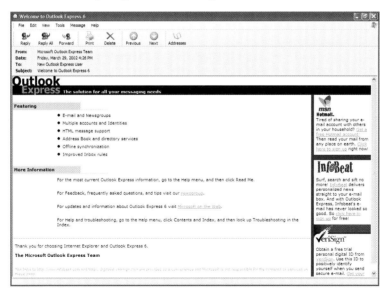

Figure 8-3 An Outlook Express message window.

When the Inbox is selected, the message window includes many of the same toolbar buttons the main Outlook Express program window displayed. These buttons perform the same functions for both windows, but in a message window, the buttons action applies only to the open message. In the Outlook Express window, the buttons act on the selected message in the message list.

Printing a Message

Printing an e-mail message is as simple as printing any other document. Just select or open the message and then click the **Print** toolbar button. If you want to change default print settings, click the **File** menu and choose **Print** to open the Print dialog box.

Deleting a Message

After you've read a message, you can decide whether you want to keep it or delete it. To delete a message that is open in its own window, click the **Delete** button in the message window's toolbar. Alternatively, you can delete messages from the Outlook Express window. To do so, select the message that you want to delete in the message list and then click the **Delete** button in the toolbar. Alternatively, you can simply press **DELETE** on your keyboard.

Deleted messages are moved to the Deleted Items folder. By default, this folder retains all deleted items until you empty it. It doesn't automatically empty itself or remove old messages unless you tell it to do so. You can recover deleted messages as long as they remain in the Deleted Items folder. To recover a deleted message, open the **Deleted Items** folder and drag and drop the message to the Inbox or to another e-mail folder.

Composing a New Message

Now that your e-mail client is configured and you know how to get around in Outlook Express, you're ready to create and send a message. To do so, perform the following steps:

If this is your first time using e-mail, compose and send a message to yourself by typing your own e-mail address in the To field in step 2. That way, you'll have an e-mail message you can use when you learn how to reply to and forward messages in the sections that follow.

① In the Outlook Express window, click **Create Mail**. The New Message window opens.
② In the To field, type the recipient's e-mail address. If the message is intended for multiple recipients, type each recipient's e-mail address, using commas or semicolons to separate them.

In the section "Using Your Address Book" later in this chapter, you'll learn how to use your address book to enter the recipient's address in the To field, as well as how to use the Cc field.

③ In the Subject field, type a meaningful subject. For example, if you're writing to a friend to invite her to dinner, you might type **Dinner** in the Subject field.

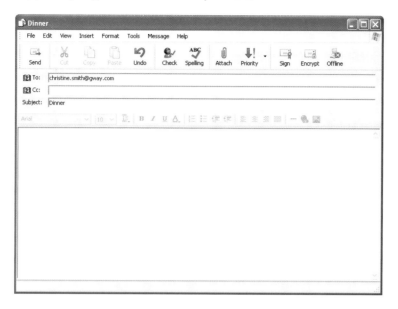

④ Type a salutation or greeting in the workspace and then type your message and name.

⑤ Click the **Send** toolbar button in the New Message window. This will either send the message immediately (if you're online) or place it in your Outbox folder.

If you're connected to the Internet, you can click the **Send** button to send the message to your outgoing e-mail server. If you're not connected, the message is placed in the Outbox folder. Messages in this folder will be sent to your outgoing e-mail server the next time you connect to that server (discussed in the next section).

To practice sending e-mails in Outlook Express, go to the Web segment *E-mail: Sending* in the Internet Explorer course.

Communicating with E-mail Servers

Just as a Web server hosts Web pages, e-mail servers support e-mail. An *e-mail server* is responsible for delivering e-mail to its intended recipient and allowing users to download their e-mail to their computers using an e-mail client. Your e-mail client handles the process of interacting with e-mail servers. All you have to do is click a single button.

To send or receive e-mail, your e-mail client must communicate with outgoing and incoming e-mail servers. Once you're online and have opened your e-mail client, a simple click of the **Send/Recv** toolbar button initiates communication. When you click the **Send/Recv** button, the e-mail client sends all messages in the Outbox to the outgoing mail server and downloads any messages waiting for you on the incoming mail server into your Inbox.

You must have an open Internet connection to send or receive e-mail. If your Internet connection is not already established, clicking the **Send/Recv** button may initiate a dial-up connection.

To test your configuration and to ensure that the message you created in the preceding section is delivered, perform the following steps:

1 Log on to your ISP or online service.

2 In Outlook Express, click **Send/Recv**. The message you sent to yourself in the preceding section should appear in your Inbox.

 If you do not see the message you sent to yourself, wait 30 seconds and repeat step 2.

Whether it's addressed to a friend up the street or a colleague on the other side of the globe, e-mail is usually delivered within seconds. However, this doesn't mean that your messages will be delivered promptly all the time. The smaller the overall size of the message, the faster it can be delivered to the recipient. If you attach a large file to a message (see "Attaching Files" later in this chapter), the message could take minutes or hours to be delivered and then, it would also take a while to download. Another factor is network traffic. Just as rush-hour traffic slows your commute to work, network traffic impedes speedy delivery of e-mail messages.

When you're online, Outlook Express automatically sends any messages you compose immediately and checks for new incoming messages every 30 minutes, by default.

Replying to a Message

If someone sends a message to which you want to reply, you can easily do so. Click either the **Reply** toolbar button (to respond only to the sender) or the **Reply All** toolbar button (to respond to the sender and any other people who received the original message). Your reply message will include the original message and any additional text you type.

To reply to a message from either the Outlook Express window or the message-display window, perform the following steps:

1. Select or open the message in your Inbox to which you want to reply. (We reply to the Welcome to Outlook Express message in this exercise.)
2. Click either the **Reply** button or the **Reply All** button. A new message window opens; notice that the To line lists all intended recipients and the original Subject line is prefixed with Re:. The message body includes a copy of the original message.

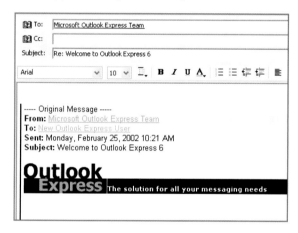

3. The blinking insertion point should already be in the upper-left corner of the message body area. If not, use your mouse to place it there, and then type your reply.
4. Click the **Send** toolbar button to send the message or place it in your Outbox.

To respond or reply to an Outlook Express e-mail you have received, go to the Web segment *E-mail: Replying* in the Internet Explorer course.

Forwarding a Message

If you receive an e-mail message containing a good joke, a great recipe, or some other interesting tidbit, you may want to forward it to a friend. When you *forward* a message, you send it to a new recipient without retyping its contents.

To forward a message either from the Outlook Express window or the message-display window, perform the following steps:

1. In your Inbox, select or open the message that you sent to yourself.
2. Click the **Forward** button. A new message window opens with a blank To line; notice that the original Subject line is prefixed with Fw:. The message body includes a copy of the original message.

3. Enter one or more e-mail addresses in the To field. For this exercise, type your own e-mail address to forward the message to yourself.
4. Click the **Send** toolbar button to send the message or place it in the Outbox.

Setting a Priority

When composing a new e-mail message, you may want to indicate to the recipient the importance of the message. The Priority feature allows you to do this. There are typically three priority levels to choose from: Low, Normal, and High. A message will default to Normal priority unless you set it otherwise. To set the priority of a message, use the Priority drop-down selection button. A message set with a High priority will appear in the recipient's e-mail client with an exclamation point. A message set with a Low priority will appear in the recipient's e-mail client with an arrow pointing down. Setting the priority does not force the recipients to read or respond to your message. It's simply an additional visual clue to get their attention.

Working with Sent Items and Drafts Folders

Besides the Inbox, Outbox, and Deleted Items folders, there are two other folders in the Folders pane of the Outlook Express window: Sent Items and Drafts.

Once a message is sent to the outgoing e-mail server, a copy of it is placed in the Sent Items folder. If you ever need to review a message or want to send the same message to someone else, you can find it in the Sent Items folder.

Some messages may take longer than others to compose. If you're interrupted halfway through the process of composing a message, you can save it in your Drafts folder until you're ready to work on it again. The Drafts folder holds a copy of any e-mail messages you're currently writing or you've written but haven't sent to the Outbox by clicking **Send**. To do so, click the **File** menu and then choose the **Save** command. When you're ready to work on the message again, simply click the **Drafts** folder to open it; your message should be displayed in the Draft folder's message list. Double-click the message to open it in its own message-display window. When you finally send the message, it will be removed from the Drafts folder.

Other E-mail Commands

If you right-click over an e-mail message, you'll see a shortcut menu. It includes several commands and functions you're already familiar with, including Open, Print, Reply to Sender, Reply to All, Forward, and Delete. It also includes additional commands that might be new to you:

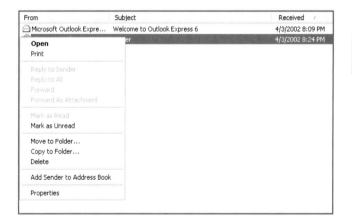

+ **Forward as Attachment.** Used to forward a message to another person. However, instead of including the text of the original message as part of the new message, the original message is added as an attachment to the forward message.

+ **Mark as Unread.** Used to mark the message as unread so it retains the bold font used on unread messages.

Mark as Unread is a useful feature for people who share an e-mail account. After the first person finishes reading a message, he or she can mark it as unread so the next person will notice the new message.

✦ **Mark as Read.** Used to remove the bold font from unread messages so they appear as read.

✦ **Properties.** Opens a dialog box that displays information about the message. Most of this information you can already view through the Outlook Express window or the open message window.

Using Your Address Book

You probably have an address book that you use to store friends' and family members' street addresses and telephone numbers. You'll want to do the same with their e-mail addresses. You can use your e-mail client's *address book* as your own personal contact list. Your address book retains all e-mail addresses you add to it, as well as other personal contact information you choose to add.

There are several ways to add contacts to your address book, but the easiest is to do the following:

1 In the message list, right-click a message you've received from the person you want to add to your list of contacts. Alternatively, if the message is displayed in its own window, right-click the person's e-mail address in the From field.

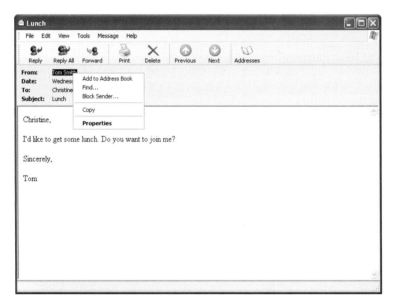

2 A shortcut menu appears. Choose Add Sender to Address Book or Add to Address Book.

Once an e-mail address is in your address book, you can quickly and easily add it to the To line of an outgoing e-mail message. Here's how:

1 Click the **To** button in the message window. The Select Recipients dialog box opens.

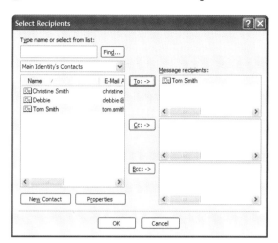

2 Click the recipient's name in the left column.

3 Click the **To: ->** button. The name now appears in the To field in the Message recipients column.

4 Click **OK**.

In step 3 you clicked the To: -> button, but notice that there are actually three buttons to choose from:

◆ **To: ->.** Click this button if the person you chose in step 2 is the message's primary recipient.

◆ **Cc: ->.** Click this button if the person you chose in step 2 should also receive the message but is not a primary recipient. For example, if you're e-mailing a co-worker about a project, you might add your boss's name to the Cc line of the e-mail message. (*Cc* stands for *carbon copy.*)

◆ **Bcc: ->.** Click this button if you want the person you selected in step 2 to receive the message but you don't want other recipients to know. (*Bcc* stands for *blind carbon copy.*)

8

To manage the contacts stored in your address book, click the **Addresses** button in the Outlook Express window or double-click a contact in the Contacts pane in the lower-left corner of the window. From the Address Book window that opens, you can create, edit, and delete contacts.

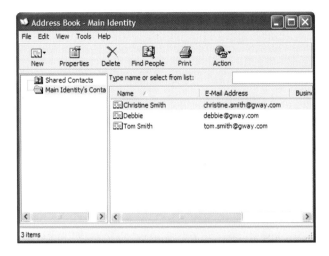

 To practice using the contact list when sending an e-mail in Outlook Express, go to the Web segment *E-mail: Using Contacts* in the Internet Explorer course.

If you find yourself sending e-mail to the same group of people often, you may want to create an e-mail group to simplify the task. Instead of having to type in or select each person's e-mail address individually, you could just select the appropriate e-mail group. An *e-mail group* is a named collection of e-mail addresses, such as your co-workers or your softball team. After you define an e-mail group, you just type the group name in the To field to send the message to everyone in the group.

To create an e-mail group, perform the following steps:

❶ Click the **Addresses** button in the main Outlook Express window.

❷ The Address Book window opens. Click **File** and then choose **New Group**.

❸ The Properties dialog box opens. On the Groups tab, type a name for this e-mail group, such as Softball or Friends.

❹ Click **Select Members**. The Select Group Members dialog box opens.

❺ Select each name and click **Select** to add it to the group. Continue to select people and click Select until you've chosen all the members for this group.

 Alternatively, you can hold down **CTRL** key while you click the names to select multiple names and then click the **Select** button.

6 Click OK. You're returned to the Properties window.

7 Review the list of group members. If you added someone's name by accident, select it and click Remove. If someone's name if missing, either use the Select Members button again or type the name and e-mail address in the fields at the bottom of the window and click Add. Click OK.

Now your group is listed as a separate contact in your address book.

Outlook Express, by default, automatically adds to your contact list (address book) the addresses of people you reply to. In other words, if you get a message from someone and click the Reply button, Outlook Express places that person's e-mail address into your contact list. This can be an excellent way to get e-mail addresses, but you may not always want an e-mail address in your contact list. You must either manually remove the unwanted contacts from your address book or disable this feature. To disable this feature, follow these steps:

1 Click Tools, and then choose Options.

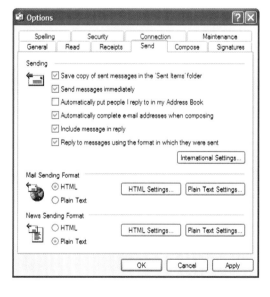

2 The Options dialog box opens. Select the Send tab.

3 Clear the check box labeled Automatically put people I reply to in my Address book.

4 Click OK.

Creating Signatures

A signature in an e-mail message is similar to the farewell and signature you'd include in a letter you'd write by hand. Once you find your friends on the Internet, you'll be creating a lot of e-mail messages. After a while, it will become tiresome to continually type in a signature at the end of each message. Most e-mail clients include a feature that will automatically insert a custom signature in each new message.

Your signature can be as basic as your name, but it can also be used to communicate contact information or messages you want your e-mail recipients to see. It's common to see e-mail addresses, URLs, addresses, phone numbers, company names, slogans, or even funny comments in a signature. You can create any kind of signature that you want.

To use the signature feature, you must first create the signature itself:

1. In the Outlook Express window, click **Tools** and then choose **Options**. The Options dialog box opens.
2. Select the **Signatures** tab.
3. Click **New**. The text Signature #1 Default signature appears in the Signatures field.
4. Select the text Signature #1.
5. Click inside the Text box below the Edit Signature heading.
6. Type a signature. You can use multiple lines if you want to.
7. When you're finished typing in your signature, select the **Add signatures to all outgoing messages** check box.

 If you don't want your signature to be added to messages you reply to or forward, select the **Don't add signatures to Replies and Forwards** check box.

⑧ Click **OK** to close the Options dialog box.

⑨ Click **Create Mail**. A new message window opens. Notice that your signature is automatically displayed as part of the message body. To type a message, just click to place the insertion point before your signature and type.

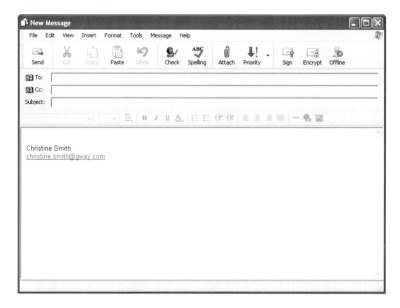

⑩ To send the message, add an address to the To line, add a subject, and click **Send**. Otherwise, click the **Close** button and click **No** to delete the message.

If you define more than one signature, you must select one of the signatures as the default. You can do so by selecting it from the list of signatures on the Signatures tab of the Option menu and clicking **Set as Default**. You can also choose to delete or rename a signature by selecting the signature and clicking **Delete** or **Rename**.

Attaching Files

An *attachment* can be any type of file—such as a document, a picture, a music file, a compressed archive, or another e-mail message—that you send over the Internet along with your e-mail message. When the recipient receives the e-mail message with the attachment, a paper clip icon appears beside the message in the message list. This indicates that one or more attachments accompany the message.

To send an attachment, perform the following:

① Click the paper clip button labeled **Attach** while creating a new e-mail message.

② The Insert Attachment dialog box opens. Use this dialog box to locate and select the file you want to attach.

③ Click **Attach**. A new line labeled Attach appears just below the Subject line in the header. This field lists the name of the file attached to the message.

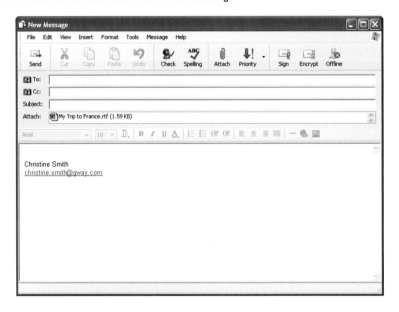

 To be able to attach documents or files to an Outlook Express e-mail message, go to the Web segment *E-mail Attachments: Adding* in the Internet Explorer course.

After the file is attached, you can either add other files as attachments or send the message (assuming you've added the recipient's e-mail address, the subject, and the body text).

Another way to add an attachment to an e-mail message is to drag and drop a file from the desktop, My Computer, or Windows Explorer onto the open New Message window. To make sure the file is attached to the message, drop it over the Attach line or the message body.

If you want to send someone an e-mail message as an attachment instead of just forwarding it, drag and drop the e-mail message from the Inbox to the open new e-mail message window. When the message you want to send is attached to the new outgoing message, it becomes a file with a .eml extension.

If you want to send someone a URL from your Favorites list, just drag and drop the Favorite from the Favorites list onto the open new e-mail message window. The URL will become a file with a .lnk extension.

When you receive e-mail with an attachment, you must first determine whether it's safe to open. You should always have anti-virus software installed and actively scanning your computer. Anti-virus software scans all incoming attachments for known viruses. With anti-virus software, most virus threats are automatically quarantined or deleted.

Here are some suggestions for determining whether an attachment is safe:

◆ If the message is from someone you don't know, delete it without opening the attachment.

◆ If the message is from someone you know but the message text is strange, includes bad grammar, or is otherwise not typical of text from that person, delete it without opening the attachment.

◆ If you receive multiple copies of the same e-mail from the same or different people, delete them without opening their attachments.

◆ If the subject line or the body text is blank, delete the message without opening the attachment.

◆ If you know the sender but were not expecting an attachment, contact the sender by e-mail or by phone to ask whether the attachment was intentional. If the sender doesn't know what you're talking about, delete it without opening the attachment.

If you think an attachment is safe because you were expecting it or because you verified that someone trustworthy sent it, go ahead and open it.

To open an attachment, follow these steps:

8

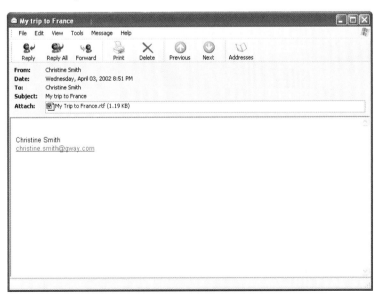

① Double-click on the message to open it.

2 Double-click on the name of an item in the Attach field to open the item.

 To practice opening attachments to an Outlook Express e-mail message, go to the Web segment *E-mail Attachments: Opening* in the Internet Explorer course.

If you don't want to open an attachment, but you want to save it to your computer, do this:

1 Double-click on the message to open it.

2 Right-click over the name of an item in the Attach field and then choose Save As. The Save Attachment As dialog box opens.

3 Use this dialog box to indicate the folder in which you want to save the attachment, such as My Documents or Desktop. You can also change the file name to something more descriptive. Click Save.

The attachment is now a file on your computer. To locate the saved file, open My Computer or Windows Explorer to navigate to the file. If you saved it to the My Documents folder, click My Documents on the start menu. If you saved it to the Desktop, double-click its name on the Desktop.

If the attachment is an e-mail message, just double-click it to open and view the message. If the attachment is an Internet link, double-click it to open it in your Web browser.

 To practice saving an attachment to an Outlook Express e-mail message, go to the Web segment *E-mail Attachments: Saving* in the Internet Explorer course.

Organizing Your E-mail

Sometimes you need to sort through your mail pile to organize and pay your bills, throw out the junk mail, and file important documents. You'll find that you occasionally need to clean out and organize your e-mail Inbox, too. Fortunately, Outlook Express offers a convenient way to file your messages so you can easily find them later. You can create new folders and subfolders underneath the Local Folders, Inbox, Outbox, Sent Items, or Draft folders. You can create your own custom hierarchy of folders to file your prized e-mails.

Generally, we recommend creating your custom folders only under the Inbox folder. Doing so prevents the top five folders from being lost in a crowd of custom folders.

You can organize folders any way you want, but an example of a possible folder hierarchy is shown in Figure 8-4. To move a message from one folder to another, just drag and drop it. Or you can right-click over a message and select the Move to Folder or Copy to Folder commands from the shortcut menu.

Figure 8-4 A sample folder hierarchy for storing e-mail messages.

Another element of keeping your e-mail organized is to delete old or unwanted messages. Periodically, review the Sent Items folder and delete any old items that you don't want to keep. If there are any messages in the Sent Items folder you want to keep, move them into other e-mail folders. You should also regularly review the contents of the Deleted Items folder and clear out messages older than three months.

It's also a good idea to review stored messages that have attachments. Large attachments take up lots of space. If you don't need to retain an attachment, delete the attachment or the entire message.

Cleaning out old and unwanted e-mail messages will keep your Inbox organized and uncluttered. Plus, it reduces the size of the storage files used by the e-mail client. Smaller working files usually result in better performance. Poor performance is most noticeable when you open or close the e-mail client.

Using Web-Based E-mail

Having a local e-mail client installed on your computer isn't the only way to send and receive e-mail. Web-based e-mail is another popular tool. Web-based e-mail is accessed from a Web site instead of from software installed on your computer. When you use Web-based e-mail, you don't have to use the same computer all the time to send and receive e-mail. Instead, you can use any computer with Internet access and a Web browser.

Several companies offer Web-based e-mail, including Yahoo! Mail and MSN Hotmail. It's very easy to sign up for a Web-based e-mail account, and they're usually free, although if you want more storage space or access to additional features, additional fees may apply.

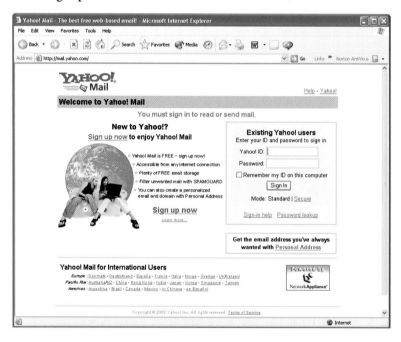

Your Web-based e-mail account will have a different e-mail address than the one assigned to you by your original ISP or online service. Each Web-based e-mail system has a unique e-mail address. For example, a Yahoo! e-mail address ends in @yahoo.com and an MSN Hotmail e-mail address ends in @hotmail.com.

Web-based e-mail gives you access to all the same functions you can perform with locally installed e-mail client software. This includes composing and sending new messages, reading messages, replying to and forwarding messages, filing messages, and sending and receiving attachments.

If you travel often or are always using different computers to connect to the Internet, Web-based e-mail may be the solution for you. Your e-mail is always accessible to you, no matter where you log on.

Go online to **www.LearnwithGateway.com** and log on to select:

- *Internet Explorer*
- *Internet Links and Resources*
  - *Newsgroups*
- *FAQs*

 With the *Survive & Thrive* series, refer to *Use and Care for Your PC* for more information on:

- *Creating folders*

 Gateway offers a hands-on training course that covers many of the topics in this chapter. Additional fees may apply. Call **888-852-4821** for enrollment information. If applicable, please have your customer ID and order number ready when you call.

8

CHAPTER 9

Communicating through the America Online Service

Whether you want to send an e-mail message to your next door neighbor, meet new people in a virtual chat room, or get involved in a discussion group with folks from all over the world, the America Online service provides you with the tools you need. In this chapter, you'll learn how to communicate with other people using the America Online service's communication tools.

Introducing America Online Communications

Besides putting information at your fingertips, the AOL service makes it possible to communicate, in some cases almost instantaneously, using tools such as Instant Messenger (often referred to as IM), newsgroups, e-mail, chat, and more. These features allow you to stay in closer contact with family, friends, and business associates, as well as make new acquaintances using the Internet. See Chapter 8 for details on newsgroups, e-mail, and chat.

AOL Instant Messenger™ enables short messages to be sent to online recipients even faster than e-mail. By using the *Buddy List*® feature, which identifies the screen names of your friends, family, and associates, you can identify when one of them is online at the same time you are and exchange messages that travel instantaneously. Please see Chapter 11 for details on Instant Messenger.

Communicating via E-mail

An e-mail address usually consists of an account name or screen name, which may or may not look like someone's real name, followed by the "at" symbol (@), followed by the Internet address of the computer handling the account's mail.

Your America Online account offers you up to seven screen names at no extra charge. Each screen name is associated with a mailbox. So, you can use different screen names for different purposes; for example, family members can have their own e-mail screen names, or you can use one address for personal use and one for business. Each of these screen names uses a different password. You must sign on separately using each screen name to send or receive e-mail from or to that screen name.

Your America Online e-mail address is the same as your screen name, followed by the "at" symbol (@), followed by aol.com.

To send a message, you must know the e-mail address of the person to whom you're sending the message. When addressing e-mail to fellow America Online members, it's not necessary to include the @aol.com after the screen name as part of the e-mail address. However, when addressing non-America Online members, the full address—for example, jsmith@anyotherserver.com—must be used.

 Don't let the high-tech terminology intimidate you. This is the same process you use to send mail today; the only difference is the tools. For example, instead of a using a pen and paper to write a message, you use your computer to type it. And instead of using the post office to deliver your message, you use the Internet.

Exploring the Structure of an E-mail Message

A simple e-mail message is composed of the *message header* and the *message body*. In the header, the author enters a brief description of the contents or purpose of the message and the e-mail addresses of all recipients. You can send an e-mail message to more than one person at a time. The message body contains the actual message.

Figure 9-1 provides a sample welcome e-mail message from the America Online administrator. Once the message is read, the recipient can choose to Keep As New, Delete the message, Forward the message to someone else, Reply to the sender, or simply do nothing and the message will move to the Old Mail tab. Reply All sends the reply message to all message recipients.

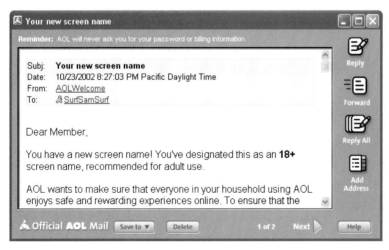

Figure 9-1 A sample welcome e-mail message.

Creating and Sending an E-mail Message

When you're creating and sending an e-mail message, using the mail buttons located in the left side of the AOL toolbar (see Figure 9-2) is probably the quickest way to execute basic mail functions. To open a blank e-mail form, click the **Write** button on the AOL toolbar.

Write Button

Figure 9-2 The mail buttons on the AOL toolbar.

 The Send To box is the equivalent of addressing an envelope. It tells the computer where the message is supposed to go. You can also launch the Write Mail window by clicking the **Mail** button on the AOL toolbar and choosing **Write Mail**.

To get started, follow these steps to create a message and send it to someone:

1 Click the **Write** button on the AOL toolbar. An empty Write Mail window opens.

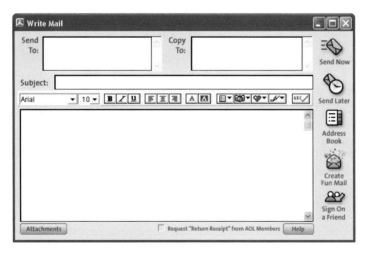

 The Copy To address box provides the same function as CC for letters. Sometimes it's necessary to share the message with other people even though they're not direct addressees.

② Click inside the **Send To** address box and type an e-mail address.

 Remember, you need only type the person's screen name; @aol.com is not required. However, if you're communicating with someone who does not use the America Online service, you'll need to include the @servername.com portion of his or her address. For example, BobSmith@gway.com.

③ Click inside the **Subject** text box and type a subject or greeting of some type.

④ Click inside the message box and type your message.

 Use the formatting toolbar to add emphasis to your text. Simply highlight the text you want to format and click the appropriate button to use a new font, add color, bold, italicize, or underline text.

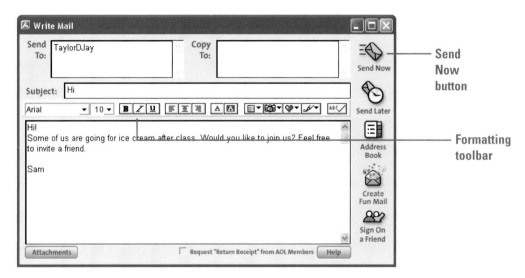

Send Now button

Formatting toolbar

9

⑤ Click **Send Now**. Your message is sent immediately.

 Clicking **Send Later** places the message in a Mail Waiting to be Sent folder in your personal file cabinet.

⑥ An acknowledgment window opens. Click **OK** to close the acknowledgment window.

 To practice sending e-mail messages with AOL, go to the Web segment *E-mail Messages: Sending* in the AOL course.

Reading and Responding to E-mail

Receiving e-mail can be as exciting as getting a letter delivered to your door! Once the letter is opened and read, you can easily reply or forward the original message to others.

Reading a Message

To learn how to read a message, follow these steps:

1 View the mail buttons on the AOL toolbar. When you have new e-mail, the Read button changes and the mailbox contains an envelope.

More About...E-mail Notification

AOL Companion provides a quick and easy way to know when you've got new e-mail messages. AOL Companion displays numbers to the right of the E-mail button (on top of the button when minimized). This number tells you at a glance how many e-mails you have waiting. You can also open your mailbox directly from AOL Companion; simply click on the mailbox icon. If you are not already logged on, you will be prompted to log on. Your mailbox will open automatically.

---

2 Look at the Welcome screen. The Mail Center hyperlink now indicates You've Got Mail.

New message icons appear as an addressed envelope. Click to open and read the message.

3 Click the **You've Got Mail** icon on the Welcome screen. The Online Mailbox window opens and contains an entry that identifies the e-mail message you just received.

④ Click Read at the bottom of the page and read the e-mail's message.

Replying to a Message

To reply to message, follow these steps:

① Click Reply to respond to the message.

② A new e-mail form appears. The original sender's address is automatically entered in the Send To address box. Notice that the Subject text remains the same but it's prefaced with the abbreviation *Re:* to indicate that it's a reply message.

 When you click Reply to respond to messages you receive from other people, the original sender's address is automatically entered in the Send To address box.

③ If necessary, click in the message body and type a reply.

④ Click Send Now and your message is sent.

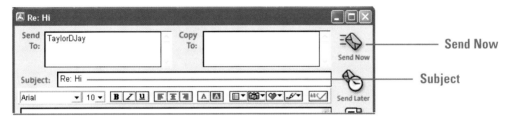

Send Now

Subject

 When corresponding with other America Online members, you can select the Request "Return Receipt" from AOL members option. A return message is sent to you when the America Online recipient has opened and read your message.

⑤ Click OK to close the acknowledgment window. Your reply has been sent. The original message window remains open on the screen.

⑥ Click on the sender's name at the top of the e-mail. The Info for dialog box for the sender's screen name appears. This gives you a number of options, including sending the sender e-mail, adding the sender to your Address Book, viewing the sender's profile, or blocking e-mail from the sender.

⑦ Click Cancel to close the Info for dialog box.

 To respond or reply to an e-mail you have received while using AOL, go to the Web segment *E-mail Messages: Replying* in the AOL course.

9

Forwarding a Message

Once you've read or replied to a message, you may want to forward it to someone else:

1 Click **Forward** to send this message to another individual. A new e-mail form appears. The Subject text remains the same, but it's prefaced with the abbreviation *Fwd*: to indicate that it's a forwarded message.

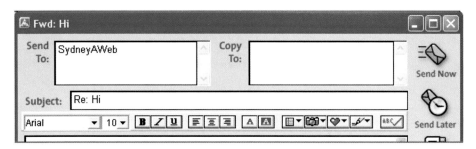

2 If necessary, click inside the **Send To** address box and type an e-mail address.

Multiple addresses can be entered into the Send To and Copy To address boxes. Type the e-mail address immediately followed by a comma, press the Spacebar, type the next address, and so on.

3 Click inside the message body and type a message.

4 Click **Send Now** and your message is sent.

5 Click **OK** to acknowledge that the message was sent as requested. The original message window remains open on the screen.

If the America Online service "Running Man" icon is present next to the screen name of the sender in an e-mail, this indicates that this person is currently online. By clicking on this person's screen name, you can quickly e-mail them or send them an Instant Message.

6 Click **Delete**.

7 You're prompted with a confirmation box asking whether you want to delete the message.

To monitor or retrieve messages that have been deleted from an e-mail account, click the **Mail** button and choose **Recently Deleted Mail**. Recently deleted mail is permanently deleted after 3-5 days.

8 Click **Yes**. The message is deleted and no longer appears on the New Mail tab in the Online Mailbox window.

9 Click the **Close** button (the button with the X in the upper-right corner of the window) to close the Online Mailbox window.

Compiling an Address Book

At this point, you may be wishing you had a place to store all your e-mail addresses. The Address Book is a helpful e-mail feature that enables America Online members to compile a listing of often-used e-mail addresses. It's fairly simple to create, edit, and delete Address Book entries:

1 Click **Mail** on the AOL toolbar and select **Address Book**. The Address Book window opens.

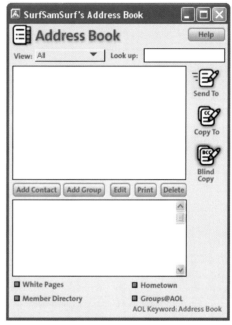

2 Click the **Add Contact** button in the middle of the Address Book window. The Contact Details dialog box opens and contains a contact information form.

3 Type a name in the **First Name** text box.

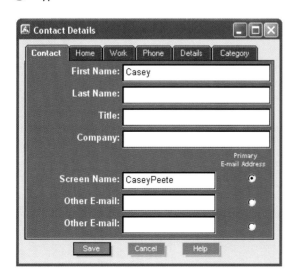

4 Type a screen name in the **Screen Name** text box if the person is an AOL user. If the user's not an AOL user, just enter the e-mail address.

5 Click the **Details** tab. This tab could contain birth dates, anniversaries, or where you met the person.

6 In the **Notes** text box, type a note about that person, for example, AOL student.

 The Notes section enables you to enter additional information that you want to remember about the person.

7 Click **Save**. The Contact Details dialog box closes the entry is added to the Address Book.

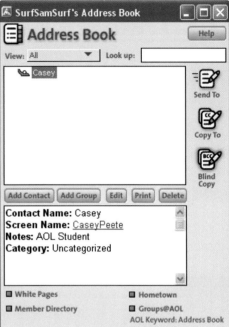

 The details of the selected entry appear in the pane on the right side of the Address Book window. If you don't want the details to appear, click **Hide Details** to hide the right pane.

8 Click **Send To** to open a Write Mail form. The e-mail address for the person selected is already in the Send To address box.

 To be able to use and add names to an AOL address book, go to the Web segment *Address Books: Compiling* in the AOL course.

Adding a Sender's Address Automatically

Upon opening and reading a message, it's possible to quickly add the address of the sender to your Address Book:

1 Click the **You've Got Mail** icon on the Welcome screen. The Online Mailbox window opens and contains an entry that identifies the reply you received.

2 Click **Read** to open the e-mail message.

3 In the open message window, click **Add Address** in the lower-right corner of the window.

4 The Contact Details dialog box opens with the Screen Name and Other E-mail text boxes automatically filled in. By default, the First Name text is highlighted.

⑤ Type the person's first name to replace the highlighted text.

⑥ Click the **Details** tab, click inside the **Notes** text box, and type a note about the person.

⑦ Click **Save** to add the entry to the Address Book.

⑧ The original message window remains open on the screen. Click the **Close** button to close the message window.

⑨ The Online Mailbox window remains open. Note that the message entry icon has changed to a red check mark to show that the message has been opened and read.

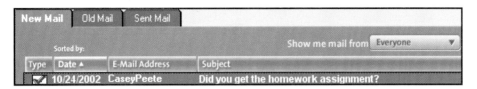

⑩ Click the **Close** button to close the Online Mailbox window.

Creating an Address Book Group

Often people will send the same message to a group of family members, friends, or colleagues. Address Book groups enable you to assign individuals to a named list, for example, golf league, kids, classmates, and so on. Individuals can belong to more than one group. To create an Address Book group, follow these steps:

① Click the **Add Group** button in the Address Book window. The Manage Group dialog box opens.

② In the section 1 text box, type a group name, such as **Classmates**.

③ In section 2, select a name, press the **CTRL** key on the keyboard, select another name, and release the **CTRL** key. Click **Add**.

In section 3, you can add contacts that are not currently in your Contact List. A comma must be placed between the e-mail addresses.

4 Click **Save** to add the new group to the Address Book.

5 The group entry is added to the Address Book window and is selected.

6 Click **Send To** to automatically open a Write Mail form that contains the addresses of those specified in the group.

The message is automatically addressed to the members of the group and ready for you to enter a subject and body text.

Attaching Files to Messages

Suppose you have a file you need to e-mail to someone; for example, maybe you have a story you wrote about your family vacation or a photograph from your vacation that you want to send to your family. It's easier and quicker to send it over the Internet than by regular mail. Files and digital photographs can be attached to e-mail messages for delivery across the Internet.

Attaching a file to an e-mail is easy, as shown in the following these steps:

1 Open a Write Mail window. (In other words, create an e-mail message to the person, or people, you would like to send the file to. Note that this message can be a reply or forward, or new message.)

2 Tab to the Subject text box and type an appropriate subject line.

3 Click the **Attachments** button in the lower-left corner of the Write Mail window. The Attachments dialog box opens.

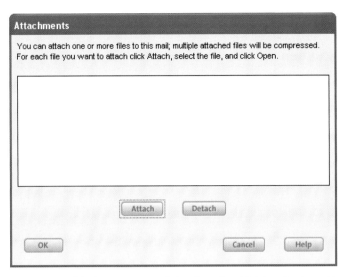

4 Click the **Attach** button. The Attach dialog box opens and prompts you to select a file. (By default, the Attach dialog box

opens with the contents of the download folder displayed.)

5 Click the **Look in** drop-down arrow and select or navigate to the folder in which the file you want to send is located.

6 Click to select the file and click **Open**.

 More than one file can be attached to a message. However, when two or more files are attached, the files are automatically zipped and the recipient of the files must have the appropriate software, such as WinZip, to decompress the files before opening them.

7 The file and its path are entered into the Attachments dialog box. Click **OK**.

8 Notice that the file is listed next to the Attachments button at the bottom of the Write Mail window.

9 Click **Send Now**. The File Transfer window briefly opens, shows the status of the file being transferred,

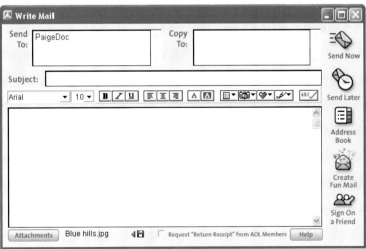

and then closes.

10 Click **OK** when the transfer is complete.

To open and read a file attachment, be aware that the recipient must have compatible software on his or her system that recognizes the file format.

 To learn how to attach documents to an AOL e-mail message, go to the Web segment *E-mail Attachments: Adding* in the AOL course.

Sending a Hyperlink

If you find an interesting Web page, area on AOL, or would like to share a favorite site with someone, it's easy to insert the page's hyperlink in an e-mail message. As discussed in Chapter 1, a URL acts as an address to define the specific name of the computer where the information is stored and the method used to access the page.

A hyperlink (also discussed in Chapter 1) is text or graphic on a page that, when clicked, opens a different object (such as a site or document), allowing you to "jump" from object to object online. For example, to send a Top News story hyperlink in an e-mail message, follow these steps:

1. Click the title bar of the Welcome screen to activate it.
2. Click the hyperlink next to the Top News section. The AOL News page opens.
3. Click one of the hyperlinks on the left side of the AOL News page.
4. Click the **Favorites** button on the title bar of the article. The America Online window opens.
5. Click **Insert in Mail**. A Write Mail form appears with an automatic entry in the Subject text box and a hyperlink to the selected site in the body of the message.
6. At this time, you will not complete or send this message. Click the **Close** button to close the Write Mail window.
7. Click **No** when the dialog box asks you if you want to save.
8. Close the AOL News page.

Reading Attachments

Suppose you receive an attachment in an e-mail message. How would you read the attachment? Attached digital files and photographs must be downloaded to a designated location to be opened and read by the associated computer application.

Locating and Opening Downloaded Files

By default, file attachments download to the C:\Program Files\America Online 8.0\download folder on your computer's hard drive. You can change that during the download process. Attached Web page hyperlinks can be accessed directly from the mail message.

Once a file is downloaded, you'll receive a Download Confirmation message confirming the download and asking if you want to locate the downloaded file immediately. If you click Yes, the America Online Service will automatically locate the downloaded file for you. To download and open a file attached to an e-mail, follow these steps:

1. Click the **You've Got Mail** icon on the Welcome Screen.
2. To indicate that a new mail message contains a file attachment, the message icon appears as an addressed envelope with a disk. Select the message with the attachment.
3. Click **Read** and read the e-mail's message.
4. Click **Download** and select **Download Now** from the pop-up menu to transfer the file to your computer. The E-mail Attachment Warning from AOL Neighborhood Watch window opens.
5. Click **Yes** if you're familiar with the sender and the source of the e-mail attachment. The Download Manager dialog box opens.

 If you do not know the sender of the e-mail message, don't download the file to your computer. E-mail attachments are a popular vehicle to transfer computer viruses to remote computers.

6. Click **Save** to download and save the file to your computer. The File Transfer window opens and closes automatically.
7. Click the **Close** button to close the window.
8. The download folder window closes

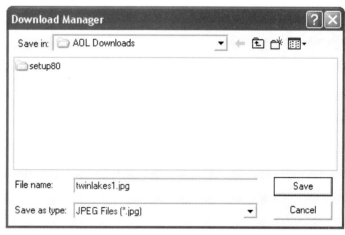

automatically.
9. The original message remains open.
10. In the see attached file window, click the **Next** arrow in the lower-right corner of the window.
11. The new message appears on the screen.
12. Click **Download** and select **Download Now**. The E-mail Attachment Warning from AOL Neighborhood Watch window opens.
13. Click **Yes** because you're familiar with the sender and the source of the e-mail attachment. The Download Manager dialog box opens.
14. Click **Save** to download and save the file to the default download directory.
15. A File Transfer window opens momentarily in the upper-left corner of the screen. The progress of

the file transfer is displayed and the window closes automatically when the transfer is complete. If your speakers are turned on, you will hear the announcement "File's done."

⑯ A preview of the file opens on top of the original message.

⑰ Click the **Close** button to close the window. The original message remains open.

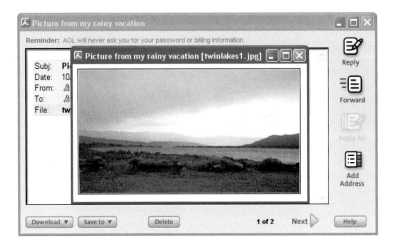

Receiving a Hyperlink

Clicking the hyperlink in an e-mail message opens the associated site in a new browser window:

❶ If necessary, open the message that contains the hyperlink.

❷ Click the hyperlink within the message body of the e-mail. The designated site opens on the screen.

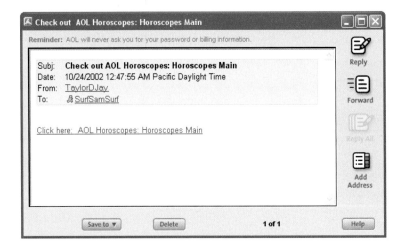

❸ Click the **Close** button to close the AOL News site. The e-mail message remains open on the screen.

❹ Click the **Close** button to close the message window.

❺ The Online Mailbox window remains open on the screen.

 The message entry icons now appear with checkmarks to indicate that the messages have been read. The messages will be transferred to the Old Mail folder for your reference the next time you click Read Mail.

❻ Click the **Close** button to close the Online Mailbox window.

Deleting Sent and Old Mail

After you've sent and received a number of e-mails, you'll notice that the content of your mailbox has grown. The Online Mailbox has several default features that help you manage your e-mail messages. Your Online Mailbox can hold up to 1,000 pieces of New Mail, 550 pieces of Old Mail, and 550 pieces of Sent Mail per screen name online at any given time. However, this mail is subject to the following time limits:

✦ **New Mail.** Unread mail remains in your New Mail list for about 27 days. After you've read an e-mail message, the AOL software automatically transfers it to your Old Mail list. To save mail as if you had not read it, click the **Keep As New** button.

 If you're a more advanced e-mail user, you can change the various default mail options to better manage your mail. For example, you can save all mail read and/or sent to your Personal Filing Cabinet on your computer's hard drive or increase the number of days (up to seven) your mail is saved online. On the browser's toolbar, open the **Settings** menu and select **Preferences**. In the Preferences window, click the **Mail** hyperlink to access other mail options.

✦ **Old Mail.** Mail remains in the Old Mail list in your mailbox for about three days.

✦ **Sent Mail.** Mail you send remains in the Sent Mail list in your mailbox for up to 27 days until your recipient reads it. After it's read, it remains in your mailbox about two days more.

Open messages and entries on the New, Old, and Sent Mail tabs can be easily deleted using the Delete button. It isn't necessary to delete mail, though, because it will be

9

automatically deleted in about three days. If you want to manually delete messages, follow these steps:

1 Click the **Read** button on the AOL toolbar. The Online Mailbox window opens. No messages appear on the New Mail tab.

2 Click the **Old Mail** tab to view the messages you have previously opened.

3 Hold down the **SHIFT** key and click the last entry in the Old Mail list. All messages are highlighted.

4 Click the **Delete** button. All entries are deleted.

5 Click the **Sent Mail** tab to view the messages you have sent previously.

6 Hold down the **SHIFT** key and click the last entry in the Sent Mail list. All messages are

highlighted.

7 Click the **Delete** button. All entries are deleted.

8 Click the **Close** button to close the Online Mailbox window.

TO KEEP ON LEARNING . . .	
	Go online to **www.LearnwithGateway.com** and log on to select: ✦ *America Online course* ✦ *Internet Links and Resources* ✦ *FAQs*
	Gateway offers a hands-on training course that covers many of the topics in this chapter. Additional fees may apply. Call **888-852-4821** for enrollment information. If applicable, please have your customer ID and order number ready when you call.

9

Chatting Online

If e-mail is the postal system of the Internet, instant messaging and chat are the equivalent of the phone system. Whereas an e-mail message is a one-way form of communication, instant messaging and chat are interactive—they allow you to carry on online conversations by sending messages back and forth to one another in real time. Instant messaging allows you to engage in a one-on-one conversation with friends, except instead of picking up the telephone, you read and write notes. Chat is similar to instant messaging in that it's interactive. However, you can converse with a whole group of people—just as if you're all on a conference call or a party line. In this chapter, you'll learn how to use these two popular means of instant online communication.

Sending and Receiving Instant Messages

With *instant messaging* (sometimes called IM), you can see whether a friend is connected to the Internet and, if so, the two of you can exchange messages. Users with instant messaging software can send messages directly back and forth to one another. The messages generally appear in small windows on each user's computer screen.

Instant messaging is different from e-mail in that the message appears on the recipient's computer as soon as it's sent. It differs from chatting in that, generally, two people are communicating rather than an entire "room" full of people sending messages back and forth. Instant messages can contain pictures and sound, as well as text.

For instant messaging to work, both users must subscribe to the same instant messaging service and must be online at the same time. In addition, the intended recipient must accept instant messages. (It's possible to set instant messaging software to reject messages, which will be covered later in this chapter.) If you attempt to send an instant message to someone who isn't online or who isn't accepting instant messages, you'll be notified that the transmission cannot be completed. If your own instant messaging software is set to accept instant messages, it alerts you with a distinctive sound or a window pops up when one has arrived, along with an option to accept or reject it. Some programs simply show a window containing the incoming message.

There are several popular instant messaging services, including Microsoft's Windows Messenger and AOL Instant Messenger. AOL Instant Messenger is covered in Chapter 11.

More About . . . Instant Messaging Software

There are dozens of instant messaging software tools. In most cases, each person you want to communicate with must either have the same instant messaging software or use one that supports the same instant messaging service. To locate other instant messaging software, perform an Internet search on "instant messaging."

Windows Messenger is present by default on Windows XP. Windows Messenger for earlier versions of Windows was known as the MSN Messenger. The applications are essentially the same, so you can use one to communicate with someone using the other.

To use the Windows messaging service, you must have a Microsoft .NET Passport account. This is a free user account established with Microsoft that grants you access to special services and Web sites. Because Windows Messenger is on all versions of Windows XP, we use it as our primary example and teaching tool for instant messaging in this chapter.

Initial Setup of Windows Messenger

To get started using Windows Messenger, perform the following steps:

10

❶ To open Windows Messenger click **start**, point to **All Programs**, and click **Windows Messenger**. The Windows Messenger window opens.

➋ Click the **Click here to sign in** link. The .NET Passport Wizard opens.

➌ Click **Next**. The Do you have an e-mail address screen appears.

➍ Assuming you have an e-mail account (which you learned how to configure in Chapter 8), select the **Yes** option.

➎ Click **Next**. The What is your e-mail address screen appears. Type your e-mail address in the E-mail Address field.

➏ Click **Next**. The Create your password screen appears. Type a password to be used when connecting to the Windows Messenger service. You must type the exact same password in both the Password and Retype Password fields.

 The Save my .NET Passport information in my Windows XP user account option is checked by default. Uncheck it if you don't want your .NET Passport information saved in your Windows XP user account.

➐ Click **Next**. The Choose and answer a secret question screen appears. The secret question will be used if you need to change your password if you forget it. Select a question from the drop-down list, and type an answer in the Answer field.

➑ Click **Next**. The Where do you live screen appears. Using the drop-down lists, select your country/region and your state (if applicable) and type your zip code.

➒ Click **Next**. The Review the .NET Passport Terms of Use screen appears. Read the agreement and click the **I accept the agreement** option.

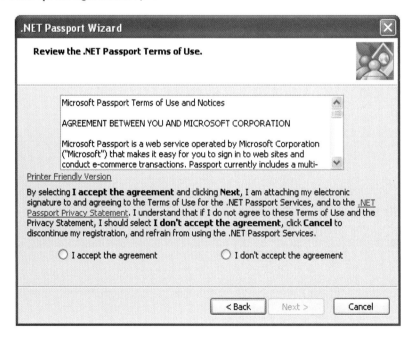

⑩ Click **Next**. The Share your information with participating sites screen appears. If you want to share your personal information with Web sites when you connect to them, select the check boxes.

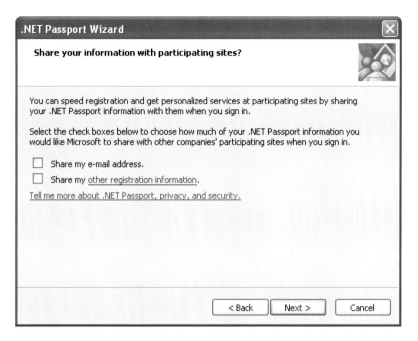

⑪ Click **Next**. The You're done screen appears.

⑫ Click **Finish** and your .NET Passport account is created.

As soon as you're finished creating a .NET Passport account, you'll be logged into Windows Messenger.

However, there's still one more step to complete before you can start using the instant messaging service. You must validate your e-mail address. Validating your e-mail address is an easy process. The instant you clicked Finish in step 12, the sign-up service sent an e-mail message to the address you provided. Just open that e-mail message, and locate the hyperlink in the paragraph that starts with "PLEASE VERIFY THAT THIS IS YOUR E-MAIL ADDRESS." Click the link. A message appears in your Web browser stating that you have just verified the e-mail address for your .NET Passport account. Now, return to Windows Messenger and perform the following:

10

① Open the **File** menu and choose **Verify My E-mail Address**.

② The Verify My E-mail Address window opens. Click **I completed the 3 steps above**.

③ You'll be logged out and presented with the Windows Messenger logon prompt. Click the **Click here to sign in** link.

Now you're verified, logged on, and ready to send and receive instant messages.

Updating Windows Messenger

As soon as you log on, see if there's a message near the top of the Windows Messenger window that states, "A new version of Windows Messenger is now available. Click here for more information." If you see that message, you can choose to update the Windows Messenger software. To update Windows Messenger, follow these steps:

① Click **A new version of Windows Messenger is now available**. Click here for more information.

② A Windows Messenger dialog box opens. Click **Yes**.

③ Click **OK**. The new software is downloaded and installed. After the process is complete, the updated Windows Messenger opens and you're automatically logged back on.

Adding Contacts

Before you can communicate with others, you have to add them to your contact list. In most cases, you simply need to provide their e-mail addresses or their Windows Messenger sign-in names. To add a contact when you know the e-mail address or sign-in name, perform the following steps:

① Click **Add a Contact**.

② The Add a Contact wizard opens. Select the **By e-mail address or sign-in name** option.

 Your contact has to be a Hotmail user or already in your local e-mail address book to use the search for contact option.

3 Click **Next**. Type the e-mail address of the contact.

4 Click **Next**. If the e-mail address is found, you'll see a success message.

5 Click **Finish**.

If the e-mail address is not found, you'll see a sorry message. Click **Back** to return to the preceding screen (step 3) and retype the e-mail address. If it fails again, you may have the wrong e-mail address for that user or that user is not using Windows Messenger. If you're sure the e-mail address is correct, the user may not use Windows Messenger. Windows Messenger prompts you to send that person an e-mail asking him or her to use Windows Messenger so you can communicate with each other via instant messages.

1 Click **Next** and type a message where indicated. Notice that there's prewritten text that will be sent to the person.

2 Click **Finish** to send the e-mail.

10

Once you've successfully added the contact to Windows Messenger, that person initially appears in the Not Online section. The contact needs to approve of receiving instant messages from you before he or she appears in your Online list.

When you're added to someone else's contact list, a dialog box appears on your screen the next time you log on to Windows Messenger. It states that someone (indicated by that person's contact e-mail address) has added you to his or her Windows Messenger contact list. You must select one of the following two options:

✦ Allow this person to see when you are online and contact you

✦ Block this person from seeing when you are online and contacting you

Selecting the first option will allow you to send and receive instant messages from this person. Selecting the second option will prevent communications. You can also select the Add this person to my contact list check box so you can initiate instant messages with this person.

Once you add someone to your contact list, your Windows Messenger window will show the contact in the Online section. Now you're all set to send and receive instant messages from your contacts.

Communicating with Instant Messages

To send an instant message to someone, he or she must be defined in your contacts list and must be online. A quick look at your Windows Messenger window will inform you whether a person is online.

To send an instant message to an online contact, perform the following steps:

❶ Click **Send an Instant Message**. The Send an Instant Message dialog box opens.

❷ Select the contact to send a message to and click **OK**. A Conversation window for that contact opens.

3 In the bottom message space, type your message.

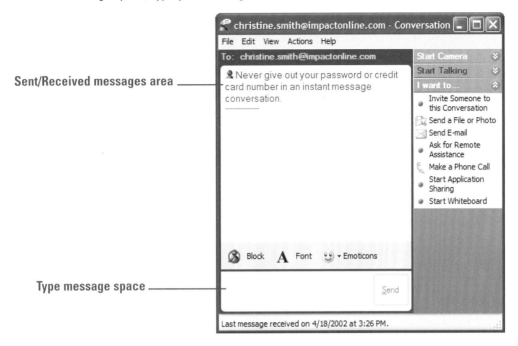

Sent/Received messages area

Type message space

4 Press **ENTER** or click **Send** to transmit the message to your contact. The sent message appears in the sent/received message area. Your e-mail address appears just above the message to indicate that it's sent by you.

If you're the receiver of an instant message, you'll hear a sound indicating that an instant message was just sent to you. A conversation dialog box opens, but it will be minimized into a button on your taskbar.

Click on the taskbar button for the conversation dialog box to open and view the received message. Once a conversation dialog box is open, you can send messages to the person who initiated the conversation. Just repeat steps 3 and 4 from the preceding exercise. When you're finishing "talking," just click the **Close** button (the button with the X in the upper-right corner) to exit the conversation dialog box.

At any time, you can double-click an online contact name in the main Windows Messenger window to open a conversation dialog box and initiate a conversation.

Sending Files via Windows Messenger

In addition to communicating with text, you can also exchange files with a contact. This can be done from the main Windows Messenger window or from a conversation window. To send a file to a contact, perform the following steps:

1 Click **Send a File or Photo**. If you started from the main Windows Messenger window, you'll need to select the contact to send the file to.

2 Select the contact and click **OK**. The Send a File to dialog box opens.

3 Locate the file to send, select it, and click **Open**.

4 A message appears in the conversation dialog box, stating that the file is queued for transmission (if the conversation dialog box was not already open, one will open).

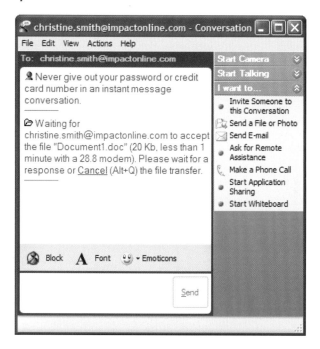

If you're the recipient of a file, you can accept or decline the offered file by clicking **Accept** (ALT+T) or **Decline** (ALT+D) in your conversation dialog box. If you accept, you'll be warned about possible transmission of viruses via file downloads (see Chapter 6). Click **OK** to continue. The file is automatically downloaded and placed in a new folder named My Received Files that is created in your My Documents folder.

Changing Your Status

Sometimes when you're online, you'll be too busy to carry on conversations with others. You can prevent others from sending you instant messages by changing your instant messaging status to temporarily appear offline or otherwise unavailable for instant messaging conversations. To change your status, click your name at the top of the Windows Messenger window and select one of the status options from the menu that appears. Your options are as follows:

◆ **Online.** You'll receive all messages.

◆ **Busy.** You'll receive messages, but the sender will receive a notice that you're unavailable to respond because you're busy and your message-received sound won't play.

◆ **Be Right Back.** You'll receive messages, but the sender will receive a notice that you're unavailable to respond and that you will do so when you return.

◆ **Away.** You'll receive messages, but the sender will receive a notice that you're unavailable to respond because you're away from your computer.

◆ **On the Phone.** You'll receive messages, but the sender will receive a notice that you're unavailable to respond because you're on the phone. Your message-received sound won't play.

◆ **Out to Lunch.** You'll receive messages, but the sender will receive a notice that you're unavailable to respond because you're out to lunch.

◆ **Appear Offline.** You won't receive messages, and the sender will receive a notice that you're offline.

Your status is automatically set to Away when you don't use Windows Messenger for 10 minutes, by default, or when your screen saver comes on. To return to normal instant message communications, reset your status to Online.

Communicating in Chat Rooms

If you like the idea of carrying on an online conversation with more than one person, you'll probably like chatting in chat rooms. They're like online coffee shops, each devoted to a particular topic, where people sit around and either make small talk or engage in extended discussions about topics of interest to them.

A *chat room* is a virtual space within the Internet where two or more users chat, or converse, in real time through messages delivered over the Internet. In a chat room, a user types a message, and the message appears on the screens of all those chatting in the room. Chat rooms often are created to support common interests such as pets, hobbies, and health concerns.

Chat rooms can also be used as lecture halls, classrooms, or presentation theaters. Special events in a chat room (typically called chat events) can give you the opportunity to communicate with or at least listen to (via reading) a famous, knowledgeable, or otherwise interesting person or group that you may not have the chance to interact with in real life.

More About... Chat Events

Want to ask two-time Tour de France champion Lance Armstrong a question about cycling? Or former Beatles member Paul McCartney about his creative process? Both celebrities have participated in online chat events, in which people asked them about their careers and personal lives. Even politicians have used chat events as a way to really connect with their constituents and find out what's on their minds.

Special chat events give anyone with an Internet connection and a Web browser the opportunity to converse with famous—and not-so-famous—people online. These chat events are advertised well in advance, and all you have to do is log on to the appropriate chat room to chat away!

To find chat rooms, use a search engine and type **chat rooms** in the search text box. A list of chat rooms will appear. Find a topic that interests you, click the link, and then click **Chat about it** or **Chat now** or something similar. There's a plethora of chat room sites on the Internet. Each chat room site may have one, dozens, or hundreds of individual chat rooms. Moving from one chat room to another on a chat room site is usually easy. However, moving from one chat room site to another chat room site can be a challenge. Just as with instant messaging software, each chat site might have unique software that is not compatible with other chat sites. The America Online service chat rooms are covered in Chapter 11.

In addition, many of the instant messaging software programs, such as Windows Messenger, have Web sites that list chat subjects and special chat events. All you have to do is click a link on the messaging software to access these sites.

One easy way to get to a chat room is to access MSN Chat through Windows Messenger. However, you must first install MSN Chat support to do so. To install MSN Chat support into Windows Messenger, perform the following steps:

❶ To open Windows Messenger click **start**, point to **All Programs**, and click **Windows Messenger**. The Windows Messenger window opens.

❷ Click the **Click here to sign in** link.

❸ Click **Go to Chat Rooms**.

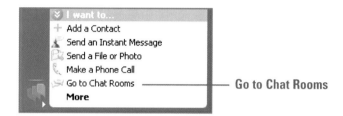

Go to Chat Rooms

❹ If this is the first time you've used Windows Messenger to enter chat rooms, you'll see a dialog box stating that an add-in to support this feature must be installed. Click **Yes**. Your Web browser opens to the Add-ins for Windows Messenger Web site.

❺ Click the **Click here to learn more!** hyperlink. The Get MSN Add-ins for Windows Messenger Web page opens.

❻ Click **Download Now!** The File Download dialog box appears.

❼ Click **Open** (do not click **Save**).

❽ Read the End-User License Agreement and then click **Yes**. A dialog box opens indicating that the add-ins were installed successfully.

❾ Click **OK**.

❿ Close any remaining open Web browser windows.

Now that MSN Chat support has been installed into Windows Messenger, you can access chat rooms through MSN Chat. To start chatting, perform the following steps:

❶ Open Windows Messenger by clicking **start**, **All Programs**, and **Windows Messenger**.

❷ Click the **Click here to sign in** link.

❸ Click **Go to Chat Rooms**. The MSN Chat window opens.

10

4 Type a nickname to use while chatting. If you can't think of a nickname, click on one of the suggested nicknames.

 It's not a good idea to use your real name or your e-mail address as your nickname. You'll need a unique nickname. If someone else is already using your nickname, you'll receive a message stating that the name is already taken and you must supply another.

 In all future chats through the MSN Chat service, it will attempt to reuse the same nickname you select here. You can change your nickname at any time.

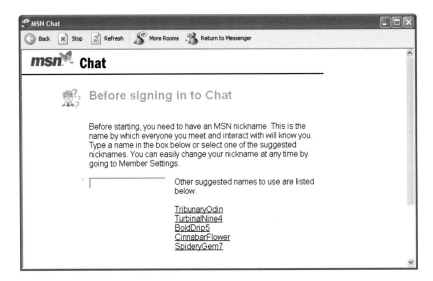

5 Scroll down and click **Register Nickname**. Once you select a unique nickname, a message confirming your nickname appears.

6 Click **Chat Now!**. A page listing all the chat rooms currently available opens. You can select from rooms devoted to different categories, such as romance, lifestyles, sports, and so on. Or you can scroll down to the bottom of the page to select a chat room by name (ordered alphabetically).

 Most chat rooms are created based on a topic or issue. It's important to stick with the topic while within a chat room. For example, don't ask for technical help with your computer in a chat room about sewing or fishing.

7 Once you find a chat room you'd like to join, click on its name. To participate in a chat room, you must download updated software. If a dialog box opens and asks you to trust downloaded content from MSN, click **Yes**. If you don't want to see that dialog box ever again, select the **Always trust content from** check box before clicking **Yes**.

8 After a few moments for downloading and installing the chat software, you may be prompted to provide your birth date. Select your birth month and day, type your birth year. Your birth date is used to determine whether you can access chat rooms meant for adults or more mature-oriented chat rooms.

10

9 Click **Continue**. After the chat software is installed, the chat room's conversation window opens.

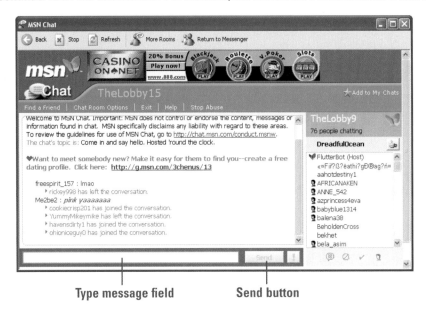

Type message field   **Send button**

Once in a chat room, you can sit and read messages from the other participants. To participate, type your message in the field at the bottom of the chat window and click **Send**. To exit a chat room, click **Exit**. You'll be shown the chat room selection screen again. When you're finished chatting, close the MSN Chat software by clicking the **Close** button.

Chat Etiquette

Just as you follow certain basic rules of etiquette when talking on the phone or talking with people in a coffee shop, it's important to follow certain rules when conversing online. *Chat etiquette* refers to the rules of etiquette you need to adhere to while participating in a public chat room. By following chat etiquette, you'll avoid inadvertently offending people and help to make the chat experience enjoyable for everyone.

As a basic rule, never say anything that you wouldn't want your mother, aunt, or clergy to hear you say. If you need more guidelines, here are some additional suggestions:

✦ Keep your conversations appropriate to the chat room's topic.

✦ Avoid mature topics and vulgar language in any chat room in which people under 18 years of age can enter.

✦ Be respectful and courteous toward the other people.

✦ Read the existing messages when you join a chat room to grasp the tone and feel of the conversation before chiming in.

- Remember that chat rooms are not private; they are public places.

- Avoid typing in all caps (for example, PLEASE LISTEN TO ME). It's considered shouting in a chat room and is usually not acceptable.

- Greet the chat room with a hello before asking questions or joining an existing conversation. Think of this as a friendly block party; you don't just walk up to a group and start talking without saying hello first.

- Be patient for a response to your messages. It may take a minute or two for others to read your post, formulate a response, and type it.

- When leaving a chat room, say goodbye or tell the people in the room that you're departing, especially if you have participated in the conversation. Before leaving, wait a few moments for goodbye responses from others.

- If you don't want to participate in the conversation but want to stay around and read what others are discussing, announce that you're just lurking. Lurking means you're going to stay in the chat room but not participate.

Finally, you should remember that even though you're using a nickname while chatting, you're not chatting anonymously. Most chat rooms record the conversations and if any illegal or questionable activities are discovered, you can be reported to the authorities.

10

TO KEEP ON LEARNING . . .

Go online to **www.LearnwithGateway.com** and log on to select:

✦ *Internet Links and Resources*

✦ *FAQs*

Gateway offers a hands-on training course that covers many of the topics in this chapter. Additional fees may apply. Call **888-852-4821** for enrollment information. If applicable, please have your customer ID and order number ready when you call.

Chatting Online Using AOL

I f you thought e-mail was the fastest way to communicate with people online, think again! With America Online's Instant Messenger and chat rooms, you can send IMs (Instant Messages) and chat with friends, family, and colleagues in real time. You can carry on an interactive conversation with other America Online service members or any Internet users who have the AOL Instant Messenger program.

In this chapter, you'll find how to communicate using AOL Instant Messenger as well as how to use AOL Instant Messenger to have conversations in chat rooms.

Communicating with AOL Instant Messenger

The America Online service provides a message service that notifies you when pre-identified users are online. Screen names are added to a Buddy List. These users can be America Online members or Internet users with AOL Instant Messenger. Short messages can be sent and received instantly among the active users, creating an online interactive conversation.

Using the Buddy List Feature

Create a Buddy List by organizing friends, family, and colleagues by interest groups or categories. The America Online service provides three existing groups: Buddies, Family, and Co-Workers.

 Think of the people you know who have a computer. Like you, they probably use the Internet to surf for information and send e-mail. There's a chance that you may be online at the same time. If this is the case, you can communicate with each other using AOL Instant Messenger.

You can also create your own custom groups by following these steps:

❶ Click the **People** button on the AOL toolbar.

❷ Choose **Buddy List** from the menu. The Buddy List window opens.

❸ Click **Setup**. The Buddy List Setup dialog box opens.

❹ Click **Add Group** to open the Add New Group dialog box.

❺ In the **Enter Group Name** text box, type a group name.

❻ Click **Save**.

❼ With the group you just added selected, click **Add Buddy** to open the Add New Buddy dialog box.

❽ In the Add New Buddy dialog box, type a screen name of someone else you know with AOL Instant Messenger.

❾ Click **Save**. The screen name is added under your new group.

 If your speakers are turned on and the person you've added is online, you'll hear the sound of a door opening.

❿ Click **Add Buddy** to open the Add New Buddy dialog box.

⓫ In the Add New Buddy dialog box, type another screen name of a friend you know who is on AOL Instant Messenger.

⓬ Click **Save**. The screen name is added under your new group.

11

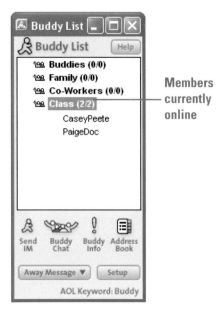

Members
currently
online

⑬ Click **Return to Buddy List**. The Buddy List window is active. Notice that your new group indicates how many members on your list are online.

 To create a Buddy List for AOL Instant Messenger, go to the Web segment *AOL Instant Messenger: Buddy List* in the AOL course.

Sending and Responding to a Message

Now that you have set up the group, you can begin sending and responding to messages. You contact a friend who's online for a one-on-one conversation using the Send IM button in the Buddy List window, as shown in the following steps:

❶ Click a screen name in the Buddy List window and click **Send IM**. The Send Instant Message window opens. In the To text box, your friend's screen name appears.

❷ Type a message and click **Send**.

 You can use the AOL Companion to send an IM right from your desktop. Simply click on the **Send IM** button in the AOL Companion to open the Send Instant Message window. If you are connected to the Internet but not already logged onto to AOL, don't worry: you will be prompted to log on, and the Send Instant Message window will open automatically.

❸ Wait for your friend to respond. If your computer's speakers are turned on, you'll hear a subtle cue to indicate that you have a message when he or she responds. View the IM From window containing the message from your friend. A message pane appears at the bottom of the IM From window.

④ Reply to the message and click **Send**.

⑤ Continue the conversation as long as you like.

⑥ When you're done chatting, click the **Close** button (the button with the X in the upper-right corner of the window) to close the IM From window.

⑦ If you choose to step away from your computer, you may wish to leave a note for anyone that may try to send you an Instant Message. To do this, click the **Away Message** drop-down menu and choose **Be Right Back**.

⑧ Your away message is displayed at the top of your Buddy List window. If other users have you listed on their Buddy List, they can read your away info by clicking their **Buddy Info** button.

⑨ To remove the away message, click the **Away Message** button. The Away Message Off dialog box opens telling you that your message has been turned off.

 Frequent users of Instant Messenger and chat often use Web-based acronyms to speed the communication process. Some examples you might encounter while communicating on the Internet are BB (bye-bye); BTW (by the way); CSG (chuckle, snicker, grin); CTN (can't talk now); LOL (laughing out loud); IMO (in my opinion); GTG (got to go); BRB (be right back); and TTYL (talk to you later).

 To practice sending a message using the AOL Instant Messenger, go to the Web segment *AOL Instant Messenger: Sending a Message* in the AOL course.

Deleting a Buddy List

If you no longer need a Buddy List, you can easily delete it:

① Click **Setup** in the Buddy List window. The Buddy List Setup window opens.

② Select the Buddy List you want to delete from the Buddy List Setup window.

③ Click **Remove**. The America Online message box appears.

④ Click **Yes**. The list is deleted from both open windows.

⑤ Click the **Close** button in the Buddy List Setup and Buddy List windows to return to the Welcome Screen.

Communicating in Chat Rooms

As mentioned previously, a chat room is a virtual space within the Internet that enables you to chat with people you know or someone you just met. AOL provides you with different ways to chat, including a Buddy List chat, public chats, and private chats. Let's first take a look at Buddy List chat.

Buddy Chat

You can chat in a private chat room by clicking the Buddy Chat button in the Buddy List window. You must first send an invitation to those you want to chat with. You can enter the screen names of those friends you want to chat with, enter a message if desired, enter the name of the private chat room, and click Send. After your buddies receive the invitation from you to chat, all you and they have to do is click Go to open the window for the appropriate private chat room and begin chatting.

In this exercise, you can learn how to use the Buddy Chat feature with a friend who is online. If your Buddy List is not already open, click the People button on the AOL toolbar and choose Buddy List from the menu, then follow these steps:

1 From your Buddy List window, click **Buddy Chat**. In the Buddy Chat window, enter the following information: In the Screen Names to Invite box, enter the friend's screen name with whom you want to chat. In the Message To Send box, use the default greeting or change it. In the Name of Private Chat Room box, edit the name of the room, if desired. Click **Send**.

 You can invite multiple friends to chat, by separating the screen names with commas.

② The person you're inviting will see an Invitation window.

Name in Chat Room window

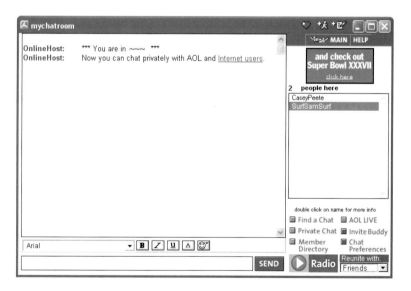

 If that person doesn't want to chat, he or she can click Cancel.

③ When the person clicks Go, a message from the OnlineHost will pop up to indicate that he or she is in the selected chat room. The OnlineHost is actually a computer. Look at the people here list on the right side of the window; it indicates who's in the chat room.

 The name of the chat room will usually be the screen name of the person sending the invitation followed by a series of numbers.

4 Use the text box at the bottom of the chat window to type a response to the message and click **Send** or press **ENTER**.

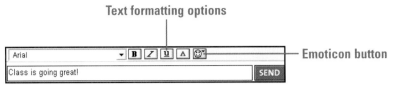

Text formatting options

Emoticon button

5 Continue responding to the messages in the chat box. Notice that as the chat box fills with messages, the text scrolls up. If you want to go back to review earlier messages, simply use the scroll bar on the right side of the chat box.

6 When you're done chatting, click the **Close** button to return to the Welcome Screen.

7 Click the **Close** button to close the Buddy List window.

Accessing Chat Rooms

If you're not sure how to get started with chat, you can use AOL People Connection:

1 On the AOL toolbar, click the **Chat** button.

2 The AOL People Connection window opens. You can use People Connection for all your chat needs. On the left side of the window, click the **Find a Chat** hyperlink.

3 The Find a Chat window opens. The chat categories are displayed in the left scroll box. The associated chat rooms are displayed in the right scroll box. In the left scroll box, select a category. Click the **View Chats** button to display the associated chat rooms in the right scroll box.

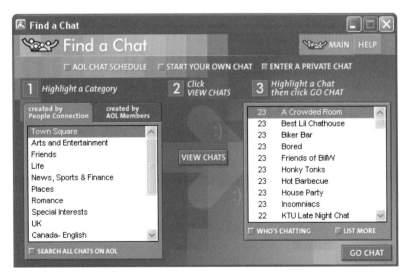

4 Scroll through the list of available chat rooms. Notice the number to the left of each chat room. That number indicates the number of people already in the chat room. If the number has reached 23, the chat room is filled.

5. Highlight the chat room you want to enter and click **Go Chat** to enter the selected chat room.

6. Once in the room, you can view the current conversations in the chat box. To chat, simply type your message in the text box at the bottom of the window and click **Send** or press **ENTER**. If you want to know who's in the chat room, look at the people list on the right side of the window. You can change the look of your text by using the font selection drop-down list and the styled text buttons.

7. When you're done chatting, click the **Close** button of all open windows to return to the Welcome Screen.

Chatting in Private Chat Rooms

You might want to create your own chat room, where you can make the chat room either a member room or a private room. A *member room* can be accessed by any member through People Connection; a private room is open only to those members who know the name of the room. You can use People Connection to begin your own chat:

1. On the AOL toolbar, click the **People** button. From the menu, choose **Start Your Own Chat**. The Start Your Own Chat window opens.

2. Click the **Private Chat** hyperlink to open the Private Chat window.

3. In the text box, type a name for your private chat room and click the **Go Chat** button to enter a private chat room. The window for your chat room opens.

4. Look at the chat room window. A message from the OnlineHost appears indicating that you're in a chat room. The OnlineHost is actually a computer. Look at the people here list on the right side of the window. It indicates who is in the chat room with you.

5. Use the text box at the bottom of the chat window to type a message or to respond to a message and click **Send** or press **ENTER**.

6. Continue responding to the messages in the chat box. Notice that as the chat box fills with messages, the text scrolls up. If you want to go back to review earlier messages, simply use the scroll bar on the right side of the chat box.

7. You may stop chatting at any time; just click the **Close** button in the chat room window and Start Your Own Chat window to return to the Welcome Screen.

 To be able to access and participate in AOL chat rooms, go to the Web segment *Chat Rooms: Accessing* in the AOL course.

11

Meeting People with AOL Match Chat™

AOL's Match Chat is a special feature which helps you easily find other people who share your interests and hobbies. To use Match Chat, you create a profile and enter information about yourself, such as your interests, hobbies, and favorite gadgets. The America Online service then matches your profile with similar profiles for you.

In this exercise, you can learn how to use Match Chat to help you find new chat buddies. Follow these steps:

❶ On the AOL toolbar, click the **Chat** button. The AOL People Connection window opens.

❷ On the left side of the window, click the **Start Match Chat™** hyperlink. The AOL Match Chat welcome window opens.

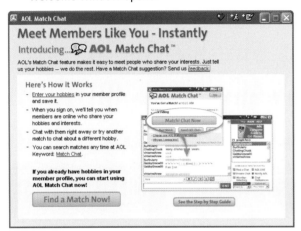

❸ In order to use Match Chat, you must first setup an AOL Member Profile. Click the **Enter Your Hobbies** hyperlink. The AOL Member Directory opens.

 Your AOL Member Profile will be available for viewing by the entire AOL community. Never post information you want to keep private, such as your full name, address, or telephone number.

❹ There are eight different categories for which you can enter information about yourself: **Name, Location, Sex, Marital Status, Hobbies & Interests, Favorite Gadgets, Occupation,** and **Personal Quote**. Click an applicable button to enter the information about yourself that you wish to share.

❺ Click the **Save** button to save your AOL Member Profile. A dialog box will inform you that your updated profile will be available in approximately an hour.

❻ In about an hour, once your AOL Member Profile has been added to the America Online service, you can return to the AOL Match Chat window and search for matches by clicking the green **Find a Match Now!** button.

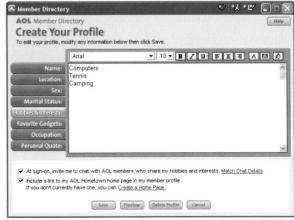

Go online to **www.LearnwithGateway.com** and log on to select:

✦ *AOL Instant Messenger: Buddy List*
✦ *AOL Instant Messenger: Sending a Message*
✦ *Chat Rooms: Accessing*
✦ *Internet Links and Resources*
✦ *FAQs*

Gateway offers a hands-on training course that covers many of the topics in this chapter. Additional fees may apply. Call **888-852-4821** for enrollment information. If applicable, please have your customer ID and order number ready when you call.

11

Account Settings and Customizations

N ow that you know how to get what you want online, you can tailor your Internet and e-mail tools to suit your individual needs and preferences. To make things as simple as possible for computer users, most Internet tools and e-mail programs use default settings. The default settings are appropriate for most users. However, as you become more skilled at surfing the Web and using e-mail, you might find that even a few simple adjustments to your Internet and e-mail tools can enrich your online experience. In this chapter, you'll find out how to make changes to suit your individual needs.

Customizing Your Web Browser

As you know, your Web browser is your window to the Internet, and the Internet Explorer Web browser allows you to add several personal touches. In the following sections, you'll find out how.

 Although you learn how to do these things in Internet Explorer in these sections, most other browsers also have similar features. Therefore, you can customize any Web browser, not just Internet Explorer.

Changing Your Home Page

The Web page that appears when you first launch Internet Explorer is called your home page. This is the default page that the browser loads each time you open it. For example, the default home page for Internet Explorer preinstalled on a Gateway computer with Windows XP Professional is **www.gatewaybiz.com**. However, as you explore the Internet, you may find another page that you'd rather have as your home page.

 Often, people choose a Web page that they use more frequently than any others as their home page. You can select any page you want as your default home page.

To change your home page, perform the following steps:

1. Click start and then click Internet.
2. If your computer doesn't connect automatically, manually establish your connection by clicking start, Connect To, and your dial-up connection.

③ Internet Explorer opens to its default home page. Open the Tools menu and choose Internet Options. The Internet Options dialog box opens.

④ If necessary, click the General tab.

⑤ In the Address text box in the Home page section, type www.gateway.net.

⑥ Click OK.

 You can use any page you want for your home page. Weather, news, and search sites are popular default home pages.

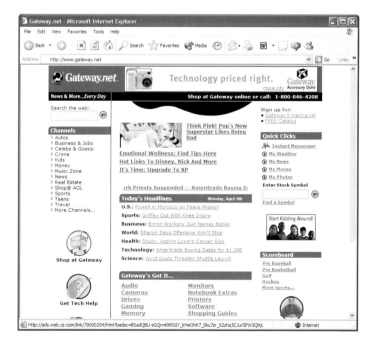

⑦ To verify your new home page setting, click the Home button. In our example, the Gateway.net site opens.

12

Now every time you open Internet Explorer, it will open to the Web page you defined as your home page.

More About . . . Setting Your Home Page

There are at least three other ways to define your home page using the General tab:

◆ Surf to the Web page that you'd like to make your home page. Open the Internet Options dialog box and click the Use Current button on the General tab. This will set your home page to the currently viewed URL.

◆ If you want to set your home page as a blank document, open the Internet Options dialog box from any Web page and click the Use Blank button on the General tab. Your new home page address will be about:blank and there will be nothing on the page.

◆ Click the Use Default button on the General tab of the Internet Options dialog box to set your home page to the computer's default. This will vary based on your computer's setup.

Managing Temporary Internet Files

You've probably already noticed that some sites take a long time to open the first time you visit them. But if you visit them again on the same day, they open quickly. Web browsers speed up your browsing by caching, or storing, Web documents, image files, and other components of a Web site on your computer temporarily.

In Internet Explorer, the cached elements are stored in the Temporary Internet Files folder. When you return to a site that has been stored as a temporary Internet file, Internet Explorer opens the temporary file (also called the local version) rather than the file on the Internet. When the local version is used, the page opens much faster but may contain old data.

Internet Explorer sets aside a certain amount of hard disk space to store temporary Internet files. You can choose how much hard disk space to make available for storing temporary Internet files and how frequently Internet Explorer checks the Web site for updates to the local versions. It's particularly useful to have your browser update temporary Internet files often if you visit sites that change constantly, such as sites that post stock reports or sports scores. If you don't refresh your temporary Internet files often enough, you might find yourself looking at a page full of old data. Internet Explorer offers several options for checking the original site for updates:

- **Every visit to the page.** The Web page is updated every time you visit it, even within a single surfing session. This option ensures that you always have the most up-to-date version of the Web page, but because the browser downloads the page from the Internet every time, it may significantly increase the time it takes the browser to load pages.

- **Every time you start Internet Explorer.** The Web page is updated every time you restart Internet Explorer.

- **Automatically.** This is the default option in Internet Explorer. If you visit a page you visited in another session or another day, Internet Explorer checks to see if the original page has changed. The Automatically setting is typically the best setting; so don't change it unless you have a good reason for doing so.

- **Never.** The Web browser always uses the stored temporary Internet file and never checks for updates. This setting is appropriate only if you don't need the updated information when a site changes or when the material on a site never changes.

To set the options for how your browser handles temporary Internet files, follow these steps:

1 From within Internet Explorer, open the Tools menu and choose Internet Options. The Internet Options dialog box opens.

2 Locate the Temporary Internet files section on the General tab.

3 Click the Settings button. The Settings dialog box opens. In this dialog box, you can specify how Internet Explorer handles temporary Internet files.

④ Notice which option is selected in the Check for newer versions of stored pages area. Select the option you've determined is most appropriate for your browsing needs.

⑤ Observe the Amount of disk space to use slider. If you have a large hard disk, you might want to use more space. The more space you allocate for temporary Internet files, the faster your computer will access Web pages that you've viewed once before.

 If you're ever running low on disk space, a temporary fix would be to lower the setting on the Amount of disk space to use slider. Usually, 35 MB is a reasonable minimum setting.

⑥ Click OK to close the Settings dialog box.

⑦ Click OK to close the Internet Options dialog box.

If you want to delete your temporary Internet files to free up some disk space or for other reasons, perform the following steps:

① From within Internet Explorer, open the Tools menu and choose Internet Options. The Internet Options dialog box opens.

② Locate the Temporary Internet files section on the General tab.

③ Click Delete Files. A Delete Files dialog box opens and asks you to confirm deletion of the temporary Internet files.

④ Select the Delete all offline content check box, and then click OK.

⑤ Once the files are deleted, you'll be returned to the Internet Options dialog box. Click OK to close the dialog box.

Blocking Cookies

Cookies are particular types of temporary Internet files that Web sites store on your hard drive. *Cookies* act as ID markers that maintain information for a specific user (or browser). This allows information for a user's preferences to be saved for subsequent visits to that site. Although cookies often benefit users by allowing them to save the content of online shopping carts and to customize Web pages they use frequently, cookies can also be used to track users' browsing habits.

You can block cookies by using Internet Explorer's Internet Options dialog box. If you choose to block cookies, any Web site you visit that requires them will respond with an error message and you'll be unable to view the page. If you want to control how cookies are used but don't want to block them altogether, you can choose to be prompted when they're used. When you choose to be prompted, a dialog box opens and asks if you wish to accept the cookie when you visit a page that utilizes them.

To configure how your browser handles cookies, follow these steps:

① Open the Tools menu and choose Internet Options. The Internet Options dialog box opens.

② Click the Privacy tab.

③ Click the Advanced button. The Advanced Privacy Settings dialog box opens.

④ Select the Override automatic cookie handling check box.
⑤ You can choose how you would like your browser to handle cookies. The default is Accept, but you can also choose Block or Prompt. Make your selection and click OK.
⑥ Click OK to close the Internet Options dialog box.

Anytime you want to delete all cookies stored by Internet Explorer, perform the following:

① From within Internet Explorer, open the Tools menu and choose Internet Options. The Internet Options dialog box opens.
② Locate the Temporary Internet files section on the General tab.

③ Click Delete Cookies. A Delete Cookies dialog box opens and asks you to confirm deletion of the cookies stored in the Temporary Internet Files folder.

④ Click OK.
⑤ Once the files are deleted, you'll be returned to the Internet Options dialog box. Click OK to close the dialog box.

12

Security Zone Settings

In addition to using appropriate virus protection software and following safe surfing habits (discussed in Chapter 6), you can protect against viruses and other damage by using your Web browser's security zone settings. *Security zones* are defined collections of Internet sites that are assigned a specific level of security. They're used to prevent damaging or untrusted content from reaching your computer. There are four security zones defined in Internet Explorer: Internet, Local intranet, Trusted sites, and Restricted sites. You use the Security tab of the Internet Options dialog box to manage the security zones.

The following list includes a description of each security zone:

+ **Internet.** Contains all sites on the Internet or local intranet that are not assigned to another zone.

+ **Local intranet.** Contains sites within your local intranet. This list is created automatically. If you're using a stand-alone computer—one that's not connected to a local network—this zone will contain only sites on your computer.

+ **Trusted sites.** Contains only sites you manually add to this zone. Sites that you fully trust can be added to this zone so you can set less-restrictive security parameters on their content.

+ **Restricted sites.** Contains only sites you manually add to this zone. Sites that you specifically don't trust can be added to this zone so you can set more-restrictive security parameters on their content.

For each zone, you can select a predefined security level or create your own custom security restrictions. The predefined security levels are High, Medium, Medium-low, and Low. The security restrictions for each level are as follows (as they appear on the Security tab of the Internet Options dialog box):

- **Low.** Minimal safeguards and warning prompts are provided; most content is downloaded and run without prompts; all active content can run; and appropriate for sites that you absolutely trust. This is the default security level of the Trusted sites zone.

- **Medium-low.** Same as medium without prompts; most content will be run without prompts; unsigned ActiveX controls will not be downloaded; and appropriate for sites on your local network (intranet). This is the default security level of the Local intranet zone.

- **Medium.** Safe browsing and still functional; prompts before downloading potentially unsafe content; unsigned ActiveX controls will not be downloaded; and appropriate for most Internet sites. This is the default security level of the Internet zone.

- **High.** The safest way to browse, but also the least functional; less secure features are disabled; and appropriate for sites that might have harmful content. This is the default security level of the Restricted zone.

To set zone security levels, follow these steps:

1. Open the Tools menu and choose Internet Options. The Internet Options dialog box opens.
2. Click the Security tab.
3. Click one of the security zone icons at the top of the dialog box.
4. Click and drag the setting slider to select the security level.

 If the setting slider is not visible but the word *Custom* is, click the Default Level button.

5. Repeat steps 3 and 4 until a security level is defined for each zone.
6. Click OK to close the dialog box.

You can also define a custom security level for each security zone. To define a custom security level, follow the preceding steps but click the Custom Level button in step 4. The Security Settings dialog box opens, and you must select a Disable, Enable, or Prompt option for each individual security control or restriction. There are over 20 individual security controls. In most cases, selecting one of the four predefined security settings is sufficient.

To add sites to the Trusted sites and the Restricted sites zones, follow these steps:

1. Open the Tools menu and choose Internet Options. The Internet Options dialog box opens.
2. Click the Security tab.
3. Click the Trusted sites icon.
4. Click Sites. The Trusted sites dialog box opens.

5. In the Add this Web site to the zone text box, type the URL for the site you want to add to the Trusted sites zone. Click Add.
6. To add another site, repeat step 5.
7. Click OK.

⑧ Click the Restricted sites icon.

⑨ Click Sites. The Restricted sites dialog box opens.

⑩ Type the URL for the site you want to add to the Restricted sites zone and then click Add.

⑪ To add another site, repeat step 10.

⑫ Click OK.

⑬ Click OK to close the Internet Options dialog box.

Managing Your Account

Just as you can customize your Web browser to suit your specific needs, you can manipulate or alter your account with some ISPs and online services. Every ISP is different, so we can't give you exact step-by-step instructions, but we can give you insight into what to look for.

The first and easiest way to discover whether your ISP or online service offers end-user account controls is to ask. If the folks at your ISP or online service don't understand what you're inquiring about, ask if you can change your password, define e-mail aliases, update your billing address, and change account services. If your ISP offers these or other services, it should provide you with a URL or other means to access account settings.

It's a good idea to keep information on contacting your ISP close at hand. We suggest writing down your ISP or online provider's name, phone numbers (voice and dial-up), primary e-mail addresses, and URLs on a note card or post-it note. Keep it near your computer just in case you need to get help and can't get online.

12

Another way to locate account settings is to access the ISP or online service's primary Web site. Look for a link labeled my account, membership controls, account preferences, and so on. If you find a link and you click it, you'll probably be asked to provide account credentials. That's just a fancy name for your user name and password that you typically use to log on when you dial up.

The following list includes some of the account settings you might find:

✦ **Change password.** You'll need to provide your old password and then type a new password twice.

✦ **Change or add e-mail aliases.** An *e-mail alias* is just another e-mail address created for your existing e-mail account. Any messages sent to an alias are automatically sent to your primary e-mail account. With aliases, you can use alternate names or e-mail addresses for different purposes. For example, if you run a small art business out of your house, you could create an alias called sales@gway.com or art@gway.com to separate the address from your personal e-mail. Some e-mail clients have the capability to separate or automatically process e-mail based on the address defined in the To line (i.e., your e-mail alias addresses).

 In most cases, you can't change your primary e-mail address because it's tied to your account name, which is a permanent, unique identifier used by the ISP or online service to differentiate your account from everyone else's.

✦ **Update billing address.** Use this type of control if you move, use an online billing service, or even change your preferred mailing addresses (such as getting a PO box).

✦ **Change account services.** Some ISPs offer different types of accounts. For example, some ISPs offer several levels of access for dial-up users, such as 30, 100, or unlimited hours, each with a different monthly or annual fee. ISPs that offer different levels of access often allow you to change your selection.

✦ **Online billing history.** Some ISPs maintain a billing history that you can view online. Often, a billing history contains a record of your dial-up connection times (similar to a phone bill statement) along with any charges or fees applied to your account.

TO KEEP ON LEARNING . . .	

 Go online to www.LearnwithGateway.com and log on to select:

◆ *Internet Links and Resources*

◆ *FAQs*

 Gateway offers a hands-on training course that covers many of the topics in this chapter. Additional fees may apply. Call 888-852-4821 for enrollment information. If applicable, please have your customer ID and order number ready when you call.

12

CHAPTER **13**

America Online Account Settings and Customizations

I n this chapter, you'll look at how you can manage and personalize your America Online service account. You'll learn about screen names, passwords, the Parental Controls feature, and how to contact America Online. You'll also examine AOL Anywhere and personalize weather, news, and portfolio information on the AOL Anywhere page.

Account Settings and Customization

Once you have used the America Online service a bit, you may have some questions about such items as your account and passwords. The America Online service offers members a robust range of member features. The Settings menu is an excellent resource from which you can access the necessary information to view your account activities, create additional screen names, set Parental Controls, and change passwords.

Adding a New Screen Name

You can have up to seven active screen names at any time: your master screen name, which you created when you registered with the America Online service, plus six others. Your master screen name cannot be deleted or changed, but other screen names can be changed and/or deleted as your situation requires. You must be connected using the master screen name to create additional screen names.

 Your screen name is your online identity. You saw it frequently when you were sending e-mail, using instant messaging, and chatting. You can change your screen name if you like.

To add a new screen name, follow these steps:

1. On the AOL toolbar, click **Settings** and choose **Screen Names**. The AOL Screen Names window opens.

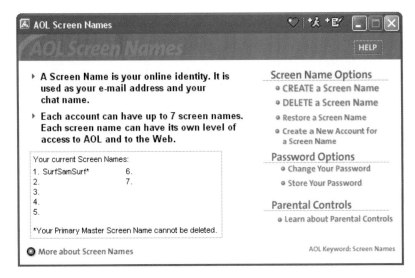

② Under Screen Name Options, click the CREATE a Screen Name hyperlink. The Create a Screen Name message box appears.

③ Click No to indicate that you're not creating the screen name for a child. The Create a Screen Name window opens. More information, including the steps for creating a screen name, appears.

④ Click the Create Screen Name button. Step 1 of 4: Choose a Screen Name opens.

⑤ Type the desired screen name in the box. Click Continue to submit the chosen screen name for uniqueness approval by the America Online service mail server.

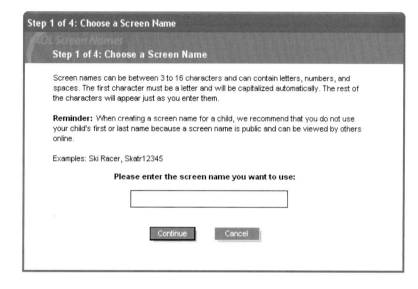

If the name you suggest is already in use, a message box appears. The mail server may suggest an available alternative name. You may accept the suggestion, or you may type in another choice.

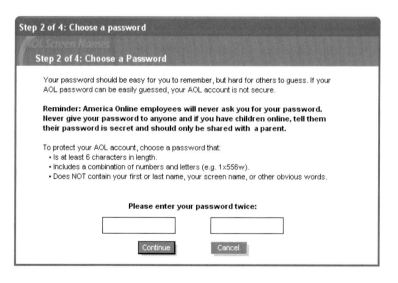

⑥ Click OK to try another name. Keep trying different names until your name is accepted. Upon acceptance of the new screen name, the Step 2 of 4: Choose a Password window opens.

⑦ Click inside the lower-left box of the Choose a Password window, if necessary, and enter a unique password. Press TAB and retype the screen name password to confirm the password.

⑧ Click Continue. The Step 3: Select a Parental Controls setting window opens.

⑨ Select General Access and click Continue. The Master Screen Name status window opens.

⑩ Verify that **No** is selected and click **Continue**. The Step 4: Confirm your Settings window opens.

⑪ Click **Accept Settings**. The AOL Screen Names window is active. Notice that the new screen name appears in the Your current Screen Names box.

⑫ Close the AOL Screen Names window to return to the Welcome Screen.

 To practice adding new AOL members or screen names, go to the Web segment *Screen Names: Adding* in the AOL course.

Changing Passwords

At some point, you may want to change your password. It's recommended that members change passwords frequently (at least monthly) to prevent unauthorized usage of accounts. A password is the key that unlocks your account and enables you to use it. If someone knows (or can figure out) your password, that's the equivalent of giving that person the key to your account. Then that person can use your account whether you permit it or not. One way to have a more secure account is to change your password frequently; for example, monthly. The America Online service also supports a "store" password feature. From the Settings menu, choose **Preferences**. In the Preferences window, click the **Passwords** hyperlink to become familiar with this option.

Follow these steps to change your password:

① On the AOL toolbar, click the **Settings** button and choose **Passwords**. The Change Your AOL Password window opens.

② Click **Change Password**. The Change Your Password dialog box opens.

③ Enter the necessary password in the Current password text box, and then enter the new password twice.

④ Click **Change Password** to activate the new password. A message box appears indicating that the password has been changed.

⑤ Click **OK** to return to the Change Your AOL Password window.

⑥ Click **Cancel** to close the Change Your AOL Password window and return to the Welcome Screen.

Exploring Parental Controls

If your children use the America Online service, you may want to set restrictions on what they can access while online. Parental Controls is a free, comprehensive feature that allows parents to assign access restrictions to the screen names they have designated for a child's use. This feature enables parents to restrict access to the Web, AOL Instant Messenger, chat rooms, e-mail, and newsgroups. You must be logged in as the master screen name to assign Parental Controls to screen names. Then follow these steps:

① Click the **Settings** button and choose **Parental Controls**. The AOL Parental Controls window opens.

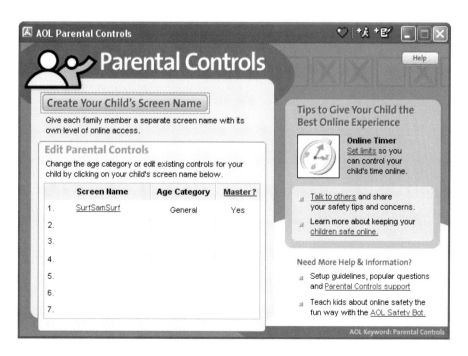

13

② Click a **Screen Name** hyperlink in the first column under Edit Parental Controls. The Parental Controls window opens.

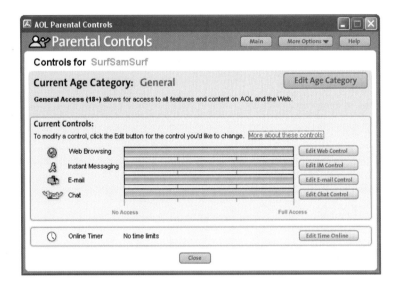

③ View the various security features available.

④ Click the **Close** button (the X in the upper-right corner of the window) in both Parental Controls windows to close them.

 To learn more about the parental controls features of AOL, go to the Web segment *Parental Controls* in the AOL course.

Switching Account Names Online

You may have multiple screen names that receive e-mail. You can switch between screen names without disconnecting from the America Online service:

① Open the **Sign Off** menu and choose **Switch Screen Name**. The Switch Screen Names dialog box opens.

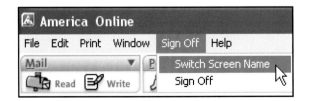

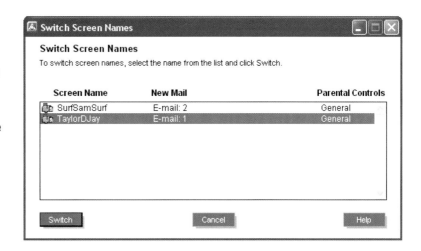

2 Select the screen name you created in the "Adding a New Screen Name" section and click the Switch button. The Switch Screen Name message box appears.

3 Click OK. The Switch Screen Name Password dialog box opens.

4 In the Password text box, type the password you assigned previously.

5 Click OK. You're notified if there's e-mail waiting.

6 Open the Sign Off menu and choose Switch Screen Name. The Switch Screen Names dialog box opens.

7 Verify that the master screen name is selected and click Switch. The Switch Screen Name message box appears.

8 Click OK and return to the Welcome Screen for the master screen name.

You may be required to type your password to return to the Welcome Screen.

Accessing Accounts and Billing Information

As with other accounts that you have, at some point you may want to know the status of your America Online account. You can easily view your account information, update your billing address, update your method of payment, and select automatic e-mail communications with appropriate departments online.

You can also use the AOL Keyword: Billing to access the AOL Billing Center.

13

To change or update billing information, you must be logged in with the master screen name. Then follow these steps:

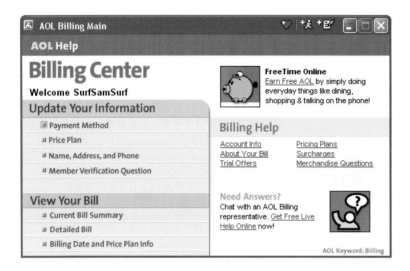

1 From the Settings menu, choose Billing Center. The AOL Billing Center window opens.

2 View the information available to you regarding your account and billing options.

 If you have additional questions about billing, call AOL customer service at 1-800-827-6364.

3 In the AOL Billing Center window, view the Frequently Asked Questions . . . (FAQs) section.

4 Click the Close button in the AOL Billing Center window to return to the Welcome Screen.

Contacting America Online

While working online, you may find that you need help. Finding the right person to help you within a large service organization can be difficult and frustrating. The America Online service alleviates the confusion by providing you with online AOL Help. To contact AOL Help, follow these steps:

1 Click the Settings button on the toolbar, and choose AOL Help. The AOL Help page opens.

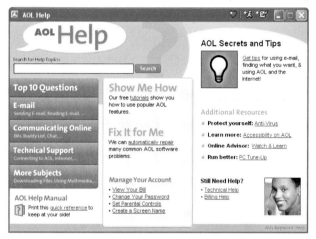

2 On the bottom right side of the window, click the Technical Help hyperlink. The Member Help Interactive Windows Technical Support page opens.

3 Click the Go There button. The AOL Live Help: Technology Help page opens.

 Screen images may be different from those pictured here.

4 If you have a question, wait until a Customer Care Consultant joins you in the chat window. If not, click Exit to leave the chat session, then click the Close button to close the window.

5 Click the Close button AOL Help window to close it.

13

Using AOL Anywhere and My AOL

AOL Anywhere is making it possible to extend the benefits of the popular AOL features and services to AOL members anywhere, anytime, and at any speed across multiple platforms and a range of devices. Members have access to the following services:

- ✦ **AOL Instant Messenger** lets you take Instant Messaging wherever you go.

- ✦ **AOL for PDAs** gives you access to your AOL from your PDA.

- ✦ **AOLbyPhone** a premium service—allows you to access AOL e-mail and more from any telephone.

- ✦ **Instant AOL** brings AOL to Internet appliances.

- ✦ **AOL.COM® service** gives you access to AOL via the AOL Web site when you're away from your computer.

- ✦ **AOL Mobile service** brings AOL to any Internet-enabled mobile phone.

- ✦ **AOL Mobile Communicator** makes it easy to exchange e-mail and IMs wherever you go.

- ✦ **T9® feature** is an easy way to enter text on a mobile phone.

- ✦ **AOL TV** lets you use your television and AOL together.

- ✦ **Wireless Alerts** provides customized info sent to any wireless device.

- ✦ The **AOL Anywhere** site

For more information, go to AOL Keyword: AOL Anywhere.

When working in a software application, many people like to personalize the environment so it best suits their needs. AOL Anywhere accomplishes this by giving you the ability to customize the America Online service using My AOL, making it easy to search and access desired information more quickly. So, when you're away from your standard AOL software/service, you can still access the information that's familiar to you and that you need. For instance, you can establish a default town/city location for daily weather updates, perform specialized news searches, and track specific stock activities.

Setting up My AOL

This exercise shows you how to use AOL Anywhere to choose a default weather forecast location:

1. On the AOL toolbar, click the AOL Keyword button.
2. Type My AOL and click Go. The My AOL page opens.
3. Scroll through the My AOL page to view the default sections.
4. Examine the Weather window of the My AOL page. Notice that your local weather forecast appears; the weather is based on the zip code you entered when you set up your AOL account.
5. In the Weather section, click the Personalize button. The Personalize menu appears.
6. Choose Customize. The Customize Weather dialog box opens.

13

⑦ In the **Add Cities** text box, type another city name, for example **San Francisco**, and click **Search**. A list of possible matches appears.appears; the weather is based on the zip code you entered on the previous screen.

⑧ Check the appropriate city name, for example, **San Francisco, CA**, and click **Save**. Now your local weather and the other city you chose appear in the Weather window.

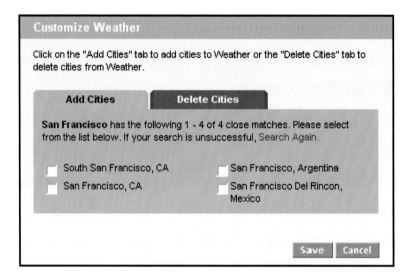

Setting up My AOL News

If you're interested in news, you can also customize the News window of My AOL:

1 Scroll to the News window on the My AOL page.

2 In the News window, click the **Personalize** button. The Personalize menu appears.

3 Choose **Customize**. The Customize News window opens.

4 In the Customize News window, place check marks in the areas of interest. You can also uncheck areas.

5 Click **Save**.

6 At the top of the My AOL page, click the **Personalize My AOL** button. The Personalize My AOL dialog box opens.

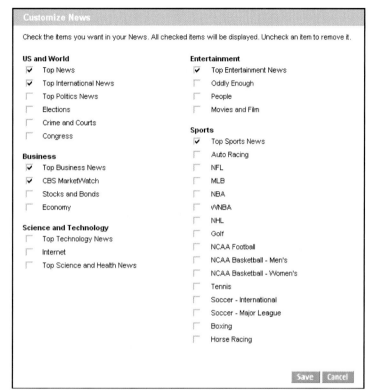

Customize News

Check the items you want in your News. All checked items will be displayed. Uncheck an item to remove it.

US and World
- ☑ Top News
- ☑ Top International News
- ☐ Top Politics News
- ☐ Elections
- ☐ Crime and Courts
- ☐ Congress

Business
- ☑ Top Business News
- ☑ CBS MarketWatch
- ☐ Stocks and Bonds
- ☐ Economy

Science and Technology
- ☐ Top Technology News
- ☐ Internet
- ☐ Top Science and Health News

Entertainment
- ☑ Top Entertainment News
- ☐ Oddly Enough
- ☐ People
- ☐ Movies and Film

Sports
- ☑ Top Sports News
- ☐ Auto Racing
- ☐ NFL
- ☐ MLB
- ☐ NBA
- ☐ WNBA
- ☐ NHL
- ☐ Golf
- ☐ NCAA Football
- ☐ NCAA Basketball - Men's
- ☐ NCAA Basketball - Women's
- ☐ Tennis
- ☐ Soccer - International
- ☐ Soccer - Major League
- ☐ Boxing
- ☐ Horse Racing

[Save] [Cancel]

7 Under Add or Remove Content, select **Calendar** and click **Save**. The Calendar window opens on the My AOL page, prompting you to set up a new Calendar if you don't already have one.

Setting up My AOL Portfolio

The Portfolio window enables you to monitor stocks and other financial funds on a regular basis. You can easily add stocks to and delete stocks from the tracking list. Follow these steps:

1 Scroll to the default Portfolio window.

2 Review the information.

3 If you know a stock or mutual fund ticker symbol, type the ticker symbol into the Enter a Ticker Symbol to Lookup Quote text box.

13

4 Click the Go button. The result of the search appears in an AOL Quotes window.

5 View the search results.

6 Click Add to Portfolio. The Add to Portfolio dialog box opens.

 If you haven't already set up a Portfolio, you'll be prompted to set one up now.

7 Click OK. A message box appears indicating that the selected stock has been added to your portfolio.

8 Click OK. The Portfolio window opens.

9 Click the Close button to close the Portfolio and AOL Quotes windows and return to the My AOL page.

10 In the Portfolio window, click the Refresh Portfolio hyperlink. A new ticker symbol is included in your portfolio list.

11 Click the Close button in all of the My AOL windows to return to the Welcome Screen.

More About…AOL Call Alert

While AOL Anywhere and My AOL give you the freedom to access AOL away from your computer, AOL Call Alert makes it easy for you to never miss a phone call when you're online at your home. AOL Call Alert notifies you of incoming calls as they happen when your residential phone line is connected to the Internet with AOL. It does this by using a feature of your telephone service known as Call Forward Busy. When someone calls you when you're online with AOL, the call is directed to AOL Call Alert. You then have the option of receiving the call, playing one of four pre-recorded messages, or ignoring the call so that you can stay online. Go to AOL Keyword: AOL Call Alert to learn how to subscribe to this premium service.

Go online to **www.LearnwithGateway.com** and log on to select:

♦ *Screen Names: Adding*

♦ *Parental Controls*

♦ *Internet Links and Resources*

♦ *FAQs*

Gateway offers a hands-on training course that covers many of the topics in this chapter. Additional fees may apply. Call **888-852-4821** for enrollment information. If applicable, please have your customer ID and order number ready when you call.

13

Troubleshooting and Getting Help

Computer and software manufacturers and ISPs (Internet service providers) have worked very hard to make connecting to the Internet as easy as possible. Typically, once your system is configured and you have an account with an ISP, all that's involved is the click of a button. But, that's not to say that connection problems won't occur. Fortunately, the problems are often simple enough for you to fix on your own. For example, you might only need to tighten a phone cord, adjust some settings, or try connecting again. Other times, you might need to seek outside professional help.

Because manufacturers and service providers want you to be able to get online easily, they provide several ways for you to get the help you need when you need it. In this chapter, we look at ways to prevent problems, examine activity status, and resolve problems when they do occur. We even provide you with a guide to finding professional help.

 This chapter is written to address problems for dial-up connections. If you have an online service provider, a cable modem, DSL, or some other type of connection, the suggestions and steps in this chapter may be different for you. Contact your service provider if this chapter doesn't apply to your situation.

Viewing Connection Status

When you connect to the Internet, a connection icon of two computer monitors typically appears in the taskbar notification area. As data is sent or received over the connection, the screens of the two monitors flash. As long as your computer is connected to the Internet, you can access Internet resources, such as Web pages and e-mail.

Connection icon

If you ever suspect that things aren't working properly, click the connection icon to open the Dial-up Connection Status dialog box, which shows the connection's status, duration, speed, and activity.

If the status is listed as disconnected, you need to reestablish your connection with your ISP or online service provider. If the status is listed as connected but you're unable to access Internet resources, disconnect and redial. To terminate an Internet connection, you can click the **Disconnect** button in the Dial-up Connection Status dialog box, or right-click the connection icon and choose **Disconnect** from shortcut menu.

Disconnect command ————

Don't be alarmed if the connection speed value is below 56 Kbps. You'll usually see a value around 28.8 Kbps. This doesn't mean that your modem is slower than it's supposed to be; it just means that the true speed of the modem is achieved through compression (i.e., compacting data before it's sent over the phone line) instead of the actual bandwidth of the dial-up connection.

In the Activity section, take a look at the number of errors listed. The errors count is a recording of the number of times a communication problem occurred and lost data had to be resent. In most cases, you can ignore this information. However, if the number of errors seems to increase rapidly (for example, if it increases several increments over a few seconds), you may have a poor telephone connection. The best way to resolve this is to disconnect and redial the connection.

Managing Your Connection

Your computer has several connection features you can use. You may also run into problems that you can fix on your own. This section will review your connection options and how you can troubleshoot connection issues.

Managing Autodialing

Your computer is capable of autodialing, which is when it automatically connects to your ISP whenever Internet access is needed. You save a few steps by having autodial enabled because you don't have to manually establish your Internet connection when you open your e-mail client or a Web browser. Autodial also has other benefits.

If your computer has anti-virus software installed, it's probably configured to periodically check for updates for its virus definitions. Autodial enables the anti-virus software to open the Internet link without you even being around.

14

The drawback to autodial is that any program set up to access the Internet can initiate an Internet connection on its own. Therefore, your computer may connect to the Internet often—even when you aren't actively using it.

As long as your ISP account is an unlimited account (i.e., you aren't limited to a specific number of hours or minutes of connection time per month), letting autodial do its thing is usually not a problem. But if you have a time-limited account, autodial can push your time usage into the extra-charges zone.

To check the autodial settings on your computer, perform the following steps:

1 Click start and then click Internet to open Internet Explorer.

2 Open the **Tools** menu and choose **Internet Options**. The Internet Options dialog box opens.

3 Click the **Connections** tab.

4 Select one of the three options in the middle of the Connections tab:

Never dial a connection. Select this option if you don't want your computer to connect to the Internet without you. If this option is selected, you'll have to manually establish an Internet connection every time you need it.

Dial whenever a network connection is not present. This option is useful only on computers that are members of a network that has shared Internet access. If you use a stand-alone computer at home, don't select this option.

Always dial my default connection. Select this option if you want to allow your computer to connect to the Internet without you. If you select this option, your computer will automatically establish an Internet connection any time you launch an Internet tool.

5 Click **OK** to close the dialog box.

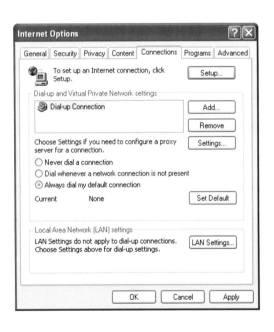

Controlling Auto-Redial

A seemingly related but distinctly different feature of connecting to the Internet is known as *auto-redial*. When auto-redial is enabled, it will automatically reestablish a connection if your computer is disconnected for any reason other than you issuing a disconnect command. Thus, if the phone company hiccups or lightning strikes in your area and your Internet connection is interrupted, your computer will immediately attempt to reconnect without you lifting a finger.

Auto-redial is not enabled by default, but it's easy to turn this feature on. To do so, just follow these steps:

❶ Click the **connection icon** in the taskbar notification area. The Dial-up Connection Status dialog box opens.

❷ Click the **Properties** button. The Dial-up Connection Properties dialog box opens.

❸ Click the **Options** tab.

❹ Select the **Redial if line is dropped** check box. This setting enables auto-redial.

❺ Set the **Redial attempts** option to the number of times you want the computer to attempt the reconnection—3 to 5 is usually an adequate range.

❻ Set the **Time between redial attempts** option to the amount of time you want the computer to wait between connection retries—1 to 3 minutes is usually an adequate range.

❼ Set the **Idle time before hanging up** option to the amount of time you want to pass before an unused Internet connection is disconnected automatically. Setting this to never means your computer will never automatically disconnect when idle. Setting this to 10 minutes means your computer will disconnect 10 minutes after the last time the Internet connection was actually used.

❽ Click **OK**.

14

Correcting Connection Problems

If your computer seems to dial and connect but you're unable to access Web pages or retrieve your e-mail, there might be problems beyond your control that you'll just have to wait for someone else to resolve. There are a few things you can try before you call your ISP. Try them in this order:

1. Disconnect and reconnect.
2. Double-check the dial-up phone number used by your Internet connection, and then try connecting again.
3. Double-check your logon user name and password, and then try connecting again.
4. Reboot your computer, and then try connecting again.
5. Change the phone cord connecting your modem to the telephone jack on the wall, and then try connecting again.

If these actions fail to establish a working connection, contact your ISP to see if there are other problems preventing you from obtaining normal Internet access.

Keep in mind that the Internet is a complicated entity—at least, the technology and components that go into creating and supporting the Internet are complex, although connecting to and using it is not. The Internet, like your cable television, electricity, and telephone services, can be susceptible to outages caused by man or nature. When things go wrong, there's little you can do but call to inform the company that there's a problem and wait until the problem is resolved.

With that said, the problem may not lie with the Internet itself, but with an electrical, telephone, or high-speed connection service.

Fortunately, serious problems with the Internet or even individual ISPs are few and far between. The few minor problems that occur are typically discovered and resolved within minutes or hours. So, if your computer seems to be working and you're able to connect to your service provider but you still can't access any online resources, call your service provider to report the problem and then wait for a bit and try again.

Mending a Bad Modem

If you've tried to resolve the problem by following the suggestions in the preceding section and you think that the problem lies with your modem and not elsewhere, there are some steps you can take. Try step 1 and then attempt to establish a connection; if that doesn't work, try step 2 and attempt to establish a connection again.

1. Replace the phone cord connecting the modem to the telephone wall jack.
2. Shut down the computer, turn off the power, wait 10 seconds, and then start the computer again.

In most cases, mending a bad modem can be resolved by updating the device driver, but this can be tricky and you should probably get professional help if it continues to fail. In rare cases, your modem may have malfunctioned because of static electricity or a flaw in its assembly. Either way, a professional can usually help resolve the problem fairly quickly. See the section "Getting Professional Help" later this chapter.

Improving Slow Connections

It's not uncommon to get a slow response when you're trying to open Web pages or download files; however, there are a few ways to improve your online experience. The most effective way is to replace your dial-up connection with a high-speed alternative such as cable or DSL (digital subscriber line).

If upgrading your connection speed is not an option, there are still a few actions you can take, but improvements gained by these actions are usually minimal:

+ Take advantage of cached files via temporary Internet files (see Chapter 12).

+ Disconnect and reconnect until you get a higher connection speed (i.e., close to or over 28.8 Kbps).

+ Wait until non-peak hours to dial in. Peak hours are typically 3 to 8 P.M. weekdays.

+ Reboot your computer and reconnect.

Using Your Computer's Help Features

If you encounter a problem that's not addressed by this chapter, you can take advantage of the troubleshooting tools built into Windows XP Help and Support Center. To access the troubleshooting section of the Help and Support Center:

❶ Click **start** and then **Help and Support**. The Help and Support Center window opens.

❷ Click the **Fixing a problem** link from the left side of the menu.

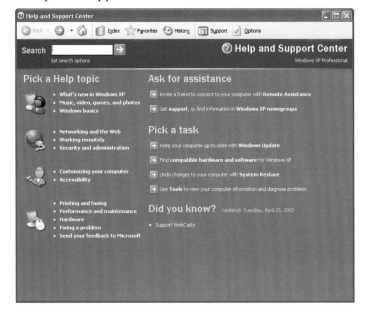

A list of problems to fix appears; the list includes problems with application and software, printing, hardware, and more. When you click one of these items, information specific to the selection appears. The information includes details on how to resolve a problem: steps to perform, tools to use, or how to launch a Windows Troubleshooter. A *Windows Troubleshooter* is a wizard that guides you through a troubleshooting process step-by-step. You can explore this information until you find what you're looking for.

If you bought your computer from a manufacturer, the help options may be a little different. For example, Gateway computers have a customized version of the Windows XP Help and Support center called the Gateway HelpSpot™.

The help information is just as extensive as the Windows XP Help and Support but it's tailored to the type of computer you own.

Getting Professional Help

Professional help is aid from any computer technician. The technician can be from any of the following:

+ Your ISP or online service provider

+ The company that sold you your computer

+ The manufacturer of your computer, individual hardware device, or specific software

+ A local repair shop

+ A dedicated technical support service

14

Be sure to have your paperwork handy, including your online service contract. You can refer to this paperwork to look up make and model information or to verify warranty coverage. If you need a technician to service your computer, be sure to give him or her a copy of that paperwork. This saves time and effort and answers many questions that might otherwise need to be asked.

It's a good idea to keep ISP or online service provider contact information close at hand. Otherwise, you'll have to hunt for it in the phone book or call information when you need it. Write your ISP or online provider's name, phone numbers (voice and dial-up), primary e-mail addresses, and URLs on a note card or post-it note. Keep this near your computer just in case you need to get help and can't get online. If your ISP can't provide the technical support you need, you can usually find technical support contact information in the phone book under "Computers."

Go online to **www.LearnwithGateway.com** and log on to select:

◆ *Internet Links and Resources*

◆ *FAQs*

 Gateway offers a hands-on training course that covers many of the topics in this chapter. Additional fees may apply. Call **888-852-4821** for enrollment information. If applicable, please have your customer ID and order number ready when you call.

14

GLOSSARY

404 error message A common Web error stating that the resource cannot be found.

500 error message A common Web error stating that the Web server cannot be reached.

address book A feature in an e-mail client program that allows you to store e-mail addresses and other personal contact information.

anti-virus software A program designed to detect malicious software present in e-mail and files copied from the Internet or across a local network. If any such software is detected or suspected, it blocks permanent storage of the infected data or puts it into a quarantine of some kind.

attachment Any type of file, such as a document, picture, music, archive, or another e-mail message, that you send over the Internet along with your e-mail message.

autodialing An Internet option that allows you to automatically connect to your ISP whenever Internet access is needed (such as when you open your e-mail client or Web browser).

auto-redial A feature that automatically reestablishes an Internet connection if your computer is disconnected for any reason other than you issuing a disconnect command.

bcc (blind carbon copy) An e-mail feature that allows you to send a copy of an e-mail message to a recipient without the recipient's e-mail address appearing in the header of the message.

Boolean operators Symbols (+, -) or words (and, or) that control the inclusion or exclusion of documents in a search.

browser controls Controls—such as the Address field, Back, Forward, Stop, Refresh, Home, and Print buttons—used by Web surfers to navigate the Internet.

cable Internet service Allows subscribers to access the Internet via cable. This shared medium, also called *high-speed broadband Internet service*, typically offers very fast throughput capabilities.

cable modem Typically an external device that uses a NIC (network interface card) to connect a computer to a cable service that offers Internet access.

cache Pronounced "cash." Web browsers speed up your browsing by caching or storing, Web documents, image files, and other components of a Web site on your computer temporarily.

cc (carbon copy) An e-mail feature that allows you to send a copy of your message to people other than the primary recipient.

chat etiquette The rules of etiquette you should adhere to while participating in a public chat.

chat room A virtual space where two or more users chat (converse) in real time through messages delivered over the Internet.

communication device A special kind of hardware that allows your computer to exchange data with other computers.

cookies Serve as ID markers for a particular user/browser so information settings can maintain continuity from one visit to the site to the next.

directory path Lists the subfolders on the Web site or Web page within which a specific resource resides.

domain name The unique text-based equivalent of a numerical IP (Internet protocol) address that is used to indicate where a particular Web resource is located on the Internet.

driver A special type of software that allows a specific hardware device to communicate with your computer.

DSL (digital subscriber line) modem Either an expansion card installed inside the computer or an external device connected to a NIC (network interface card) that is used to connect a computer to a digital phone service that offers Internet access.

DSL (digital subscriber line) A dedicated medium that gives users high-speed Internet access via digital telephone service.

eBooks Consist of the text of a book in a special file that is formatted so it looks like a printed book, but is viewed on a computer or hand-held computer screen. Also called *electronic books*.

e-mail account A service you get from an ISP or online service that supplies you with a unique e-mail address and allows you to send and receive e-mail messages.

e-mail address A unique address you use to send and receive e-mail messages. Typically, the format is the user name, followed by the @ symbol, and then the domain name.

e-mail client program A program used to send and receive e-mail.

e-mail group A named collection of e-mail addresses, such as addresses for your co-workers or your softball team.

e-mail message Written communication, similar to a letter, that is sent from one computer to another. Also called *electronic mail*.

e-mail server A computer responsible for delivering e-mail to its intended recipient and allowing users to download their e-mail to their computer using an e-mail client.

e-mail service types The standard mail servers used to send and receive mail on the Internet are POP3 (Post Office Protocol 3), IMAP (Internet Message Access Protocol), and HTTP (Hypertext Transfer Protocol).

e-mail signature The personalized closing text of an e-mail message, similar to the farewell and signature you'd include in a handwritten letter.

encrypt A security feature that uses SSL (Secure Sockets Layer) to encode and protect personal information sent between your Web browser and another computer.

firewall A piece of software or hardware that can selectively block access to your computer from unauthorized outsiders.

FTP (File Transfer Protocol) client A dedicated FTP tool used to upload and download files over a network.

FTP (File Transfer Protocol) A system whereby users can transfer files over a network.

home page A predefined Web site that your Web browser loads each time it opens.

HTML (Hypertext Markup Language) The most common markup language used to create Web pages.

HTTP (Hypertext Transfer Protocol) The computer language of the Web.

hyperlinks Text or graphical elements on a Web page that you can click to go to another Web page. Also called *links*.

IMAP (Internet Message Access Protocol) mail server One of the standard mail servers used to send and receive mail on the Internet.

Inbox The area in which new messages sent to your e-mail address appear when they're downloaded to your computer.

instant messaging Sending messages directly back and forth between users with instant message software when both parties are online and available. Also called *IM*.

instant messenger programs Programs that enable people to send short messages to online recipients even faster than e-mail.

Internet A physical network of millions of computers around the world. This network allows the computers to communicate back and forth. Also called the *information superhighway*.

IP (Internet protocol) address The unique numerical equivalent (such as 216.52.41.129) of a text-based domain name used to indicate where a particular Web resource is located on the Internet.

ISP (Internet service provider) A company that provides Internet access to subscribers.

ISP (or online service) account A service contract with an ISP or online service that defines what type of connection may be used and how many hours the connection can be active per month before extra charges apply.

keyword A word that describes the topic you want to search for on the Internet.

mail server A computer that manages all of an ISP or online service's incoming and outgoing mail messages.

markup language A specialized language used to create Web pages by defining the layout of the text and graphics.

member room A chat room that can be accessed by any members of that particular Web site.

message body The actual information contained in an e-mail.

message header A brief description of the contents or purpose of the message and the e-mail addresses of all recipients.

message list pane Specific information about e-mails—such as the sender, message subject, and date and time received—displayed in the window's upper-right pane.

modem A device that allows a computer to communicate or exchange data with other computers using a standard phone line.

network Two or more computers connected by communication devices, such as a phone line or cable and a NIC, so they can exchange files and other data. *See NIC.*

newsgroups Online discussion groups whose members post articles and messages that pertain to specific topics of interest.

NIC (network interface card) Pronounced "nick." This device permits a computer to access a network, and because some networks are themselves connected to the Internet, to use that connection for Internet access as well. Also called a *network adapter.*

online catalog Usually a collection of the products sold by a store, with pictures, descriptions, and prices of the items.

online game Any game you play on the Internet, whether it's a single-player game or involves many people from all over the world.

online purchase protection A benefit that allows you to dispute a charge on your credit card from any online store.

online service A company that provides Internet access to members or subscribers.

POP3 (Post Office Protocol 3) mail server One of the standard mail servers used to send and receive mail on the Internet.

port address Tells your browser exactly from what location to request its resource.

preview pane A feature of most e-mail client programs that allows you to quickly preview e-mail messages in the Inbox window's bottom pane without opening (double-clicking) a specific e-mail.

primary master account Used to establish a connection between your computer and the ISP or online service. Also referred to as a *master screen name.*

private chat room An invitation-only virtual space within the Internet where two or more users chat (converse) in real time through messages delivered over the Internet.

protocol language The set of rules and standards that allows computers to communicate.

quarantine option A feature of most anti-virus software; this option saves infected files to a special directory on your computer.

resource name The actual name of the file containing the Web page or other resource that the URL identifies.

safe surfing Habits that will help keep your computer safe from viruses because you'll avoid places where you're most at risk of getting them.

screen name A unique online identity you create to establish an e-mail account or Internet account, or to access restricted information on the Web.

search engine An Internet program that performs its search against Internet content. It uses automated software tools known as spiders, robots, or crawlers to create and maintain a database of information about the Internet. The spiders, robots, or crawlers download nontrivial content from every single Web page they can find on the Internet.

search tool A utility on a Web site that searches all or part of the Internet using keywords and other information you supply.

secondary (or individual) accounts Allows family members or other individuals to establish their own e-mail addresses and online identities separate from the primary master account.

security zone Defined collections of Internet sites that are assigned a specific level of security, such as Internet, local intranet, trusted sites, and restricted sites. Used to prevent damaging or untrusted content from reaching your computer.

SMTP (Simple Mail Transfer Protocol) mail server The standard outgoing mail server used on the Internet.

SSL (Secure Sockets Layer) Used to encode and protect personal information sent between your Web browser and another computer.

subject directory Searches against an internal subject catalog (typically separated by categories), which is a database that is maintained on the directory site itself.

surfing the Web Entering URLs and clicking hyperlinks to explore various Web sites on the Internet.

throughput The speed at which a communication device, such as a modem, sends and receives data; measured in Kbps (kilobits per second), Mbps (megabits per second), or Gbps (gigabits per second).

Trojan horse A kind of computer "infection" that can illicitly damage your computer while purporting to run a legitimate activity.

URL (uniform resource locator) A special kind of Internet address that defines the route to the requested information. The URL consists of up to six parts—the protocol language, domain name, port address, directory path, resource name, and spot marker.

virtual checkout The Internet equivalent of the checkout line at a grocery store where you "take" your items to be purchased.

virtual shopping cart The Internet equivalent of a shopping cart at the grocery store. As you explore an online store, you place items that you want to purchase into the shopping cart.

Web browser Software used to access the Web. Also called a *browser*.

Web page A document formatted for viewing over the Internet through a Web browser.

Web server A computer on the Internet that houses one or more Web sites.

Web site A collection of online documents maintained by an individual or a group.

Web-based e-mail E-mail accessed from a Web site instead of from software installed on your computer.

World Wide Web A vast collection of interconnected graphical and textual information that exists because the Internet provides a foundation for it. Often just called the *Web*.

Index

A

accounts
  customizing, 234–37
  Internet access, 16–24,
    229–30, 234–37
  managing, 229–30
  at online stores, 49
  setting up, 16–24, 25, 30,
    234–37
  See also passwords; screen
    names
Acrobat Reader, 99, 100, 107–9,
  113
Add Buddy button, 209
Add Contact button, 175
Add Group button, 177
Add to Portfolio window, 246
Address bar, 8, 32, 37, 123, 124
Address Books
  creating, 175–78
  saving e-mail addresses in,
    154–57
  window for, 175, 176, 177,
    178
address field, 30–32, 34, 38
Adobe Acrobat Reader, 99, 100,
  107–9, 113
aliases, e-mail, 229–30
Amazon.com, 8, 47–49
anti-virus software, 103, 104–7
  See also viruses
Anywhere feature, 242–46
Anywhere Help, 132–33
AOL (America Online)
  account setup, 16–24, 30,
    234–37 (*See also*
    accounts)
  basic description of, 6, 16
  billing information, 239–40
  customer service, 16, 52–53,
    54, 239, 241

customizing, 220–31, 234–46
exploring, 119–38
screen names, 18, 121,
  168–69, 175, 238–39
Toolbar, AOL, 122–23, 134,
  208, 243
Welcome screen, 122, 123,
  126–27, 137, 172
See also AOL (America
  Online) buttons; AOL
  (America Online)
  channels; AOL (America
  Online) features; AOL
  (America Online)
  windows
AOL (America Online) buttons
  Add Buddy, 209
  Add Contact, 175
  Add Group, 177
  Attachments, 178–79
  Away Message, 211
  Back, 31, 32–33, 40, 83–85,
    123
  Buddy Chat, 212
  Buddy Info, 211
  Change Zip Code, 125
  Details tab, 176
  Favorite Place, 136
  Favorites, 133–35, 180
  Forward, 30–33, 123
  Go, 124
  Home, 30–32, 33
  Insert in Mail, 180
  Keyword, 123, 243
  Keyword List, 137
  Maximize, 32, 125
  Minimize, 32
  Open Content Drawer, 124,
    125
  People, 208
  Personalize, 242–46
  Print, 30–31, 33, 34, 91, 148

Read, 184
Refresh, 30–31, 32, 40, 123
Reload, 40
Restore, 32
Search, 124, 138
Select This Screen, 127
Send IM (Instant Message),
  210
Send Later button, 171
Send Now, 171, 173, 174
Sign On, 121
Sports Scores, 127
Start, 17, 19, 120
Stop, 30–31, 32, 33, 123
Weather, 125
Write, 170
AOL (America Online) channels
  Auto, 128
  Careers & Work, 52–53, 128
  Computer Center, 128
  Entertainment, 128
  Games, 129
  Health, 129
  House & Home, 129
  International, 129
  Kids Only, 129
  Local Guide, 129
  Music, 130
  News, 130
  Parenting, 130
  Personal Finance, 130
  Research & Learn, 130
  Shopping, 131
  Sports, 131
  Teens, 131
  Travel, 132
  Welcome, 132
  Women's, 132
AOL (America Online) features
  Anywhere feature, 242–47
  Better on AOL Broadband,
    126

HTTP (Hypertext Transfer
        Protocol), 36, 37, 96,
        145
hyperlinks
    Autos hyperlink, 138
    basic description of, 7, 8, 39
    Buyers Guides hyperlink, 138
    color of, 39
    e-mailing, 90–91, 180
    graphical, 39
    receiving in e-mail, 182–83
    selecting, 7
    underlined, 39
    See also URLs (Uniform
        Resource Locators)

I

images
    albums, online, 64
    downloading, 114–16
    file types, 99
    GIF (Graphics Interchange
        Format) files, 99, 115
    JPEG (Joint Photographic
        Experts Group) format,
        99, 101, 115
    sending, via e-mail, 64, 115
    TIFF (Tagged Image File
        Format), 99, 115
    wallpaper, 115
    Web sites, photo-sharing, 64
    You've Got Pictures™
        feature, 16, 126
    See also downloading files
Insert in Mail button, 180
instant messages (online),
        188–98
Instant Messenger™, 16, 142,
        174, 234
    AOL Companion and, 124
    basic description of, 168
    sending and receiving
        messages, 210–11
    See also chats
International Channel, 129

Internet
    account setup, 15–24
    basic description of, 2–4
    cable access to, 13–15, 101,
        126, 250, 255
    dial-up access to, 15–24, 41,
        101, 251, 259
    DSL access to, 14, 15, 101,
        126, 250, 255
    getting connected to, 11–26,
        251–52
    reconnecting to, 41
    resources on, overview, 4–5
    terminating connection to,
        23, 41
    the World Wide Web and, 5,
        6
    See also browsers; ISPs
        (Internet Service
        Providers)
Internet Explorer (Microsoft)
        browser
    basic description of, 6, 32–35
    Content Advisor, 67–70
    customizing, 220–25
    downloading files with, 95,
        108, 111, 115–16
    e-mail features, 90–91
    entering URLs with, 38
    error messages and, 40–41
    Favorites feature, 35, 86–91
    file formats and, 99, 100
    search engines, using, 81–83
    Windows XP and, 6, 30–31
IP (Internet Protocol) addresses,
        36, 37, 145
IRS (Internal Revenue Service)
        Web site, 78, 80, 96,
        107
ISPs (Internet Service Providers)
    account management
        features, 229–30
    account setup features, 15–24
    basic description of, 5, 7, 16
    e-mail services provided by,
        144, 145, 150, 164

technical support from, 253,
        257–58
    See also Internet; online
        services

J

JPEG (Joint Photographic
        Experts Group) format,
        99, 101, 115
    See also images

K

KB (kilobytes), 12
keywords
    Keyword button, 123, 243
    Keyword List button, 137
    searching for, on Web pages,
        34
    searching with, 76, 79–80,
        136–38
    useful keywords
        AOL Anywhere, 242
        AOL Call Alert, 246
        Digital City, 129
        Guarantee, 131
        Help, 132
        PF (personal finance), 130
        Quick Checkout, 131
        Reminder, 131
kids
    homework help, 129, 130
    homework help for, 71
    Parental Controls for, 16,
        67–70, 234, 235–36
Kids Only Channel, 129

L

LearnWithGateway.com, 9
links
    See hyperlinks
Local Guide Channel, 129

M

Mail button, 170
Mail Center, 126, 172, 174

GATEWAY, INC. END-USER LICENSE AGREEMENT

IMPORTANT - READ CAREFULLY: This End-User License Agreement (EULA) is a legal agreement between you (either an individual or an entity), the End-User, and Gateway, Inc. ("Gateway") governing your use of any non-Microsoft software you acquired from Gateway collectively, the "SOFTWARE PRODUCT".

The SOFTWARE PRODUCT includes computer software, the associated media, any printed materials, and any "online" or electronic documentation. By turning on the system, opening the shrinkwrapped packaging, copying or otherwise using the SOFTWARE PRODUCT, you agree to be bound by the terms of this EULA. If you do not agree to the terms of this EULA, Gateway is unwilling to license the SOFTWARE PRODUCT to you. In such event, you may not use or copy the SOFTWARE PRODUCT, and you should promptly contact Gateway for instructions on returning it.

SOFTWARE PRODUCT LICENSE

The SOFTWARE PRODUCT is protected by copyright laws and international copyright treaties, as well as other intellectual property laws and treaties. The SOFTWARE PRODUCT is licensed, not sold.

1. **GRANT OF LICENSE.** This EULA grants you the following rights:
   - **Software.** If not already pre-installed, you may install and use one copy of the SOFTWARE PRODUCT on one Gateway COMPUTER, ("COMPUTER").
   - **Storage/Network Use.** You may also store or install a copy of the computer software portion of the SOFTWARE PRODUCT on the COMPUTER to allow your other computers to use the SOFTWARE PRODUCT over an internal network, and distribute the SOFTWARE PRODUCT to your other computers over an internal network. However, you must acquire and dedicate a license for the SOFTWARE PRODUCT for each computer on which the SOFTWARE PRODUCT is used or to which it is distributed. A license for the SOFTWARE PRODUCT may not be shared or used concurrently on different computers.
   - **Back-up Copy.** If Gateway has not included a back-up copy of the SOFTWARE PRODUCT with the COMPUTER, you may make a single back-up copy of the SOFTWARE PRODUCT. You may use the back-up copy solely for archival purposes.

2. **DESCRIPTION OF OTHER RIGHTS AND LIMITATIONS.**
   - **Limitations on Reverse Engineering, Decompilation and Disassembly.** You may not reverse engineer, decompile, or disassemble the SOFTWARE PRODUCT, except and only to the extent that such activity is expressly permitted by applicable law notwithstanding this limitation.
   - **Separation of Components.** The SOFTWARE PRODUCT is licensed as a single product. Its component parts and any upgrades may not be separated for use on more than one computer.
   - **Single COMPUTER.** The SOFTWARE PRODUCT is licensed with the COMPUTER as a single integrated product. The SOFTWARE PRODUCT may only be used with the COMPUTER.
   - **Rental.** You may not rent or lease the SOFTWARE PRODUCT.
   - **Software Transfer.** You may permanently transfer all of your rights under this EULA only as part of a sale or transfer of the COMPUTER, provided you retain no copies, you transfer all of the SOFTWARE PRODUCT (including all component parts, the media and printed materials, any upgrades, this EULA, and the Certificate(s) of Authenticity), if applicable, and the recipient agrees to the terms of this EULA. If the SOFTWARE PRODUCT is an upgrade, any transfer must include all prior versions of the SOFTWARE PRODUCT.
   - **Termination.** Without prejudice to any other rights, Gateway may terminate this EULA if you fail to comply with the terms and conditions of this EULA. In such event, you must destroy all copies of the SOFTWARE PRODUCT and all of its component parts.
   - **Language Version Selection.** Gateway may have elected to provide you with a selection of language versions for one or more of the Gateway software products licensed under this EULA. If the SOFTWARE PRODUCT is included in more than one language version, you are licensed to use only one of the language versions provided. As part of the setup process for the SOFTWARE PRODUCT you will be given a one-time option to select a language version. Upon selection, the language version selected by you will be set up on the COMPUTER, and the language version(s) not selected by you will be automatically and permanently deleted from the hard disk of the COMPUTER.

3. **COPYRIGHT.** All title and copyrights in and to the SOFTWARE PRODUCT (including but not limited to any images, photographs, animations, video, audio, music, text and "applets," incorporated into the SOFTWARE PRODUCT), the accompanying printed materials, and any copies of the SOFTWARE PRODUCT, are owned by Gateway or its licensors or suppliers. You may not copy the printed materials accompanying the SOFTWARE PRODUCT. All rights not specifically granted under this EULA are reserved by Gateway and its licensors or suppliers.

4. **DUAL-MEDIA SOFTWARE.** You may receive the SOFTWARE PRODUCT in more than one medium. Regardless of the type or size of medium you receive, you may use only one medium that is appropriate for the COMPUTER. You may not use or install the other medium on another COMPUTER. You may not loan, rent, lease, or otherwise transfer the other medium to another user, except as part of the permanent transfer (as provided above) of the SOFTWARE PRODUCT.

5. **PRODUCT SUPPORT.** Refer to the particular product's documentation for product support. Should you have any questions concerning this EULA, or if you desire to contact Gateway for any other reason, please refer to the address provided in the documentation for the COMPUTER.

6. **U.S. GOVERNMENT RESTRICTED RIGHTS.** The SOFTWARE PRODUCT and any accompanying documentation are and shall be deemed to be "commercial computer software" and "commercial computer software documentation," respectively, as defined in DFAR 252.227-7013 and as described in FAR 12.212. Any use, modification, reproduction, release, performance, display or disclosure of the SOFTWARE PRODUCT and any accompanying documentation by the United States Government shall be governed solely by the terms of this Agreement and shall be prohibited except to the extent expressly permitted by the terms of this Agreement.

7. **LIMITED WARRANTY.** Gateway warrants that the media on which the SOFTWARE PRODUCT is distributed is free from defects in materials and workmanship for a period of ninety (90) days from your receipt thereof. Your exclusive remedy in the event of any breach of the foregoing warranty shall be, at Gateway's sole option, either (a) a refund of the amount you paid for the SOFTWARE PRODUCT or (b) repair or replacement of such media, provided that you return the defective media to Gateway within ninety (90) days of your receipt thereof. The foregoing warranty shall be void if any defect in the media is a result of accident, abuse or misapplication. Any replacement media will be warranted as set forth above for the remainder of the original warranty period or thirty (30) days from your receipt of such replacement media, whichever is longer. EXCEPT AS EXPRESSLY SET FORTH HEREIN, GATEWAY, ITS SUPPLIERS OR LICENSORS HEREBY DISCLAIMS ALL WARRANTIES, EXPRESS, IMPLIED AND STATUTORY, IN CONNECTION WITH THE SOFTWARE PRODUCT AND ANY ACCOMPANYING DOCUMENTATION, INCLUDING WITHOUT LIMITATION THE IMPLIED WARRANTIES OF MERCHANTABILITY, NON-INFRINGEMENT OF THIRD-PARTY RIGHTS, AND FITNESS FOR A PARTICULAR PURPOSE.

8. **LIMITATION OF LIABILITY.** IN NO EVENT WILL GATEWAY, ITS SUPPLIERS OR LICENSORS, BE LIABLE FOR ANY INDIRECT, SPECIAL, INCIDENTAL, COVER OR CONSEQUENTIAL DAMAGES ARISING OUT OF THE USE OF OR INABILITY TO USE THE SOFTWARE PRODUCT, USER DOCUMENTATION OR RELATED TECHNICAL SUPPORT, INCLUDING WITHOUT LIMITATION, DAMAGES OR COSTS RELATING TO THE LOSS OF PROFITS, BUSINESS, GOODWILL, DATA OR COMPUTER PROGRAMS, EVEN IF ADVISED OF THE POSSIBILITY OF SUCH DAMAGES. IN NO EVENT WILL GATEWAY, ITS SUPPLIERS' OR LICENSORS' LIABILITY EXCEED THE AMOUNT PAID BY YOU FOR THE SOFTWARE PRODUCT. BECAUSE SOME JURISDICTIONS DO NOT ALLOW THE EXCLUSION OR LIMITATION OF LIABILITY FOR CONSEQUENTIAL OR INCIDENTAL DAMAGES, THE ABOVE LIMITATION MAY NOT APPLY TO YOU.

9. **Miscellaneous.** This Agreement is governed by the laws of the United States and the State of South Dakota, without reference to conflicts of law principles. The application of the United Nations Convention on Contracts for the International Sale of Goods is expressly excluded. This Agreement sets forth all rights for the user of the SOFTWARE PRODUCT and is the entire agreement between the parties. This Agreement supersedes any other communications with respect to the SOFTWARE PRODUCT and any associated documentation. This Agreement may not be modified except by a written addendum issued by a duly authorized representative of Gateway. No provision hereof shall be deemed waived unless such waiver shall be in writing and signed by Gateway or a duly authorized representative of Gateway. If any provision of this Agreement is held invalid, the remainder of this Agreement shall continue in full force and effect. The parties confirm that it is their wish that this Agreement has been written in the English language only.

"Rev.3 9/24/98".

Mission

Deep inside one of America's leading computer companies is a group of very smart, very dedicated people who have nothing to do with designing or manufacturing computers. Their special mission to help you unlock the power of your computer, to achieve your fullest potential. With fresh insights and breakthrough techniques, the Survive & Thrive series will transform the way you learn about technology. And put a human face on the digital revolution. Yours.

Online Learning Subscription

Flexible and affordable, Online Learning gives unlimited access, anytime, anywhere. With one click, you get cutting-edge curriculum, message boards & online community.

Learning for your lifestyle
- Discover Digital Music and Photography
- Brush up your software skills
- Power your productivity

Start anytime - learn anywhere

www.LearnwithGateway.com

Learning Library

Delivering the benefits of classroom learning experience without the classroom, Gateway's Learning Library provides a step-by-step approach using powerful CD-ROMs to allow you to learn at your own pace, on your own schedule.

Offers include the following Learning Libraries:
- Microsoft Office XP Professional (Also in Spanish!)
- Microsoft Works Suite